THE ULTIMATE
NEW YORK METS
TRIVIA BOOK

A Collection of Amazing Trivia Quizzes
and Fun Facts for Die-Hard Mets Fans!

Ray Walker

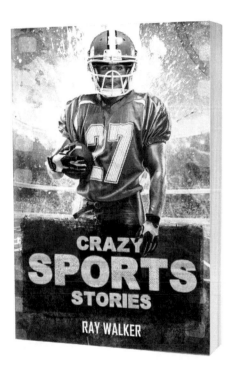

CONTENTS

INTRODUCTION

The New York Mets were established in 1962 as an expansion team to replace the Dodgers and Giants in New York. The Mets have proven themselves to be a team that fights hard and is a force to be reckoned with in MLB.

They have won two World Series championships, in 1986 and 1969, and they have also won the National League pennant five times. They are very often a threat in the National League East Division, having won it six times so far. They also have earned three wild card berths.

The Mets have retired the uniform numbers of Tom Seaver, Mike Piazza, Casey Stengel, and Gil Hodges. They also have a New York Mets Hall of Fame at Citi Field to celebrate their past and the players and people who made it all possible.

The thing about baseball is that it is a lot like life. There are good times and bad times, good days and bad days, but you have to do your absolute best to never give up. The New York Mets have proven that they refuse to give up and that they will do anything they need to do in order to bring a championship to Queens. Winning is more than possible when you have a storied past, as the Mets do. They have so much captivating history and so many undeniable player legacies to be profoundly proud of.

The Mets' current home is Citi Field, which opened in 2009. They play in one of the most difficult divisions in baseball, the National League East, alongside the Atlanta Braves, Miami Marlins, Philadelphia Phillies, and Washington Nationals.

With such a storied team past that goes back generations, you're probably already very knowledgeable as the die-hard Mets fan that you are. Let's test that knowledge to see if you truly are the World's Biggest Mets fan.

CHAPTER 1:

ORIGINS & HISTORY

QUIZ TIME!

1. Which of the following team names did the Mets franchise once go by?

   a. Yankees

   b. Giants

   c. Bulldogs

   d. They have always been the Mets

2. In what year was the New York Mets franchise established?

   a. 1901

   b. 1955

   c. 1962

   d. 1969

3. The Mets' current home stadium is Citi Field.

   a. True

   b. False

4. Which division do the New York Mets currently play in?

    a. American League Central
    b. American League East
    c. National League East
    d. National League Central

5. The New York Mets have never won a wild card berth.

    a. True
    b. False

6. How many National League pennants has the Mets franchise won (as of the 2020 season)?

    a. 3
    b. 5
    c. 9
    d. 12

7. What is the name of the Mets' mascot?

    a. Mets Mackaw
    b. Mets Man
    c. Met Monkey
    d. Mr. Met

8. Who is the longest-tenured manager in New York Mets history (as of the 2020 season)?

    a. Terry Collins
    b. Yogi Berra
    c. Bobby Valentine
    d. Davey Johnson

9. What is the name of the New York Mets' Triple-A Team and where is it located?

   a. Louisville Bats
   b. Gwinnett Stripers
   c. Syracuse Mets
   d. Norfolk Tides

10. Who was the first manager of the Mets?

   a. Wes Westrum
   b. Joe Frazier
   c. Gil Hodges
   d. Casey Stengel

11. The Mets were founded as an expansion team to replace the Dodgers and Giants who had both moved to California.

   a. True
   b. False

12. What is the name of the Mets' current spring training home stadium?

   a. Publix Field
   b. Clover Park
   c. CoolToday Park
   d. JetBlue Park

13. How many appearances has the New York Mets franchise made in the MLB playoffs (as of the 2020 season)?

   a. 9
   b. 11

c. 14

d. 18

14. How many World Series titles have the Mets won (as of the 2020 season)?

    a. 1

    b. 2

    c. 3

    d. 4

15. The Mets used to play in the American League East Division from 1962-1969.

    a. True

    b. False

16. Which stadium was the first home stadium of the New York Mets franchise?

    a. New York Stadium

    b. Shea Stadium

    c. Yankee Stadium

    d. Polo Grounds

17. As of the 2020 season, how many National League pennants have the Mets won?

    a. 3

    b. 5

    c. 7

    d. 9

18. How many National League East Division titles have the Mets won (as of the 2020 season)?

a. 6

b. 11

c. 15

d. 18

19. Which team is NOT currently in the National League East Division alongside the Mets?

    a. Miami Marlins

    b. Washington Nationals

    c. Philadelphia Phillies

    d. Chicago Cubs

20. Of all the teams in the NL East, the Mets have won the division the most times.

    a. True

    b. False

QUIZ ANSWERS

1. D – They have always been the Mets

2. C – 1962

3. A – True

4. C – National League East

5. B – False (3)

6. B – 5

7. D – Mr. Met

8. A – Terry Collins

9. C – Syracuse Mets

10. D – Casey Stengel

11. A – True

12. B – Clover Park

13. A – 9

14. B – 2

15. B – False (They have always been in the National League East Division.)

16. D – Polo Grounds

17. C – 7

18. A – 6

19. D – Chicago Cubs (They were a founding member of the NL East but moved to the NL Central in 1994.)

20. B – False (Atlanta Braves)

DID YOU KNOW?

1. The Mets have had 22 managers: Casey Stengel, Wes Westrum, Salty Parker, Gil Hodges, Yogi Berra, Roy McMillan, Joe Frazier, Joe Torre, George Bamberger, Frank Howard, Davey Johnson, Bud Harrelson, Mike Cubbage, Jeff Torborg, Dallas Green, Bobby Valentine, Art Howe, Willie Randolph, Jerry Manuel, Terry Collins, Mickey Callaway, and Luis Rojas. Carlos Beltran was hired as manager for the 2020 season but resigned before it began due to his role in the Houston Astros' cheating scandal.

2. The Mets' current manager is Luis Rojas. He is the son of former MLB manager Felipe Alou and the half-brother of former MLB outfielder, Moises Alou.

3. Davey Johnson is the New York Mets' all-time winningest manager with a record of 595-417, a .588 W-L%.

4. Casey Stengel was the first to have his number retired by the New York Mets. His number 32 was retired in 1965.

5. The New York Mets have hosted two MLB All-Star Games, the first in 1964 at Shea Stadium and the second in 2013 at Citi Field.

6. Mets pitchers have thrown only one no-hitter.

7. A perfect game has never been thrown by a Met pitcher.

8. The Mets' Double-A team is the Binghamton Rumble Ponies.

9. Mr. Met is believed to be the first mascot in Major League Baseball to exist in human form. Mrs. Met is often seen with Mr. Met, as well.

10. In 2019, Forbes ranked the Mets as the 38th most valuable sports team in the world and the 6th most valuable team in the MLB.

CHAPTER 2:

JERSEYS & NUMBERS

QUIZ TIME!

1. The Mets colors combine Dodgers blue and Giants orange to represent the fact that the Mets replaced them in New York.

    a. True
    b. False

2. In 1998, the color _____ was added to the Mets' color scheme. It was completely phased out by 2013.

    a. Green
    b. Yellow
    c. Red
    d. Black

3. For the 2014 season, a Mr. Met sleeve patch was added to the Mets' blue alternate jerseys. It was phased out by 2017.

    a. True
    b. False

4. Which of the following numbers has NOT been retired by the New York Mets (as of the end of the 2020 season)?

   a. 31
   b. 34
   c. 37
   d. 41

5. What uniform number does 1B Pete Alonso currently wear?

   a. 10
   b. 15
   c. 20
   d. 25

6. What uniform number did slugger Mike Piazza wear during his time with the Mets?

   a. 25
   b. 31
   c. 33
   d. 35

7. The Mets' cap has an orange interlocking "NY" logo, identical to the New York Giants' (MLB) logo. The logo is on a blue cap reminiscent of the caps worn by the Brooklyn Dodgers.

   a. True
   b. False

8. Which of the players below is NOT one of the three New York Mets players who have worn the uniform No. 0?

    a. Terry McDaniel

    b. Rey Ordoñez

    c. Tony Clark

    d. Omar Quintanilla

9. Which former Mets manager has his No. 14 retired by the team?

    a. Joe Torre

    b. Yogi Berra

    c. Casey Stengel

    d. Gil Hodges

10. The Mets' primary logo was designed by sports cartoonist, Ray Gotto.

    a. True

    b. False

11. What are the New York Mets' official team colors?

    a. Blue and orange

    b. Blue, orange, and white

    c. Blue, orange, and black

    d. Blue, orange, white, and black

12. Who was the first Met to have his uniform number retired by the team?

    a. Mike Piazza

    b. Gil Hodges

    c. Tom Seaver

    d. Casey Stengel

13. C Mike Piazza is the latest to have his number (31) retired by the Phillies, on July 30, 2016.

    a. True

    b. False

14. What jersey number did Tom Seaver wear as a Met?

    a. 21

    b. 31

    c. 41

    d. 51

15. What jersey number did Dwight Gooden wear as a Met?

    a. 11

    b. 16

    c. 17

    d. 21

16. What jersey number did David Wright wear as a Met?

    a. 2

    b. 3

    c. 4

    d. 5

17. What jersey number does Jacob deGrom currently wear for the Mets?

    a. 38

    b. 40

    c. 48

    d. 50

18. What jersey number did Darryl Strawberry wear as a Met?

    a. 17

    b. 18

    c. 26

    d. 39

19. What jersey number did Al Leiter wear as a Met?

    a. 22

    b. 25

    c. 26

    d. 28

20. The Mets currently have retired the numbers of two players and two managers (as of the end of the 2020 season).

    a. True

    b. False

QUIZ ANSWERS

1. A – True

2. D – Black

3. A – True

4. B – 34

5. C – 20

6. B – 31

7. A – True

8. C – Tony Clark (He wore No. 00.)

9. D – Gil Hodges

10. A – True

11. B – Blue, Orange, White

12. D – Casey Stengel (1965)

13. A – True

14. C – 41

15. B – 16

16. D – 5

17. C – 48

18. B – 18

19. A – 22

20. A – True

DID YOU KNOW?

1. Each part of the NYC Skyline in the Mets' primary logo has a meaning. At the left is a church spire, symbolic of Brooklyn. The general skyline view represents the Empire State Building, while the far right showcases the United Nations headquarters. The bridge in the center represents the Mets, who brought National League baseball back to New York. It also represents all five boroughs of New York.

2. Blue and orange represent the Dodgers and Mets, but they are also the colors of New York City as shown on its flag.

3. The only one player who has ever worn No. 99 for the Mets is Turk Wendell, from 1997 to 2001.

4. The Mets currently have one standard batting helmet design that they wear with every uniform. In the past, they had different batting helmets to match whichever uniform they were wearing for that game.

5. The Mets' white pinstriped uniforms replaced both their cream pinstriped uniform and their alternate white uniform starting in the 2015 season.

6. The Mets have retired four numbers, representing Gil Hodges (No. 14), Mike Piazza (No. 31), Casey Stengel (No. 37), and Tom Seaver (No. 41). Jerry Koosman is expected to have his number retired by the Mets next season.

7. Jackie Robinson's No. 42 is retired by the Mets as well as the MLB as a whole. No Mets or MLB player will ever wear No. 42 again. The Yankees' Mariano Rivera was the last player to wear it.

8. Four players have worn No. 73 for the Mets: Kenny Rogers (1999), Ricardo Rincon (2008), Robert Carson (2012-2013), and Daniel Zamora (2018-2019).

9. Carlos Gomez is the only player to have worn No. 91 for the Mets in franchise history. He wore it during the 2020 season.

10. Mr. Met wears No. 00. Mrs. Met wears No. 00 as well.

CHAPTER 3:

FAMOUS QUOTES

QUIZ TIME!

1. Which former Mets pitcher once said: "You have the honor and privilege of being in position to do something amazingly special. If you have the chance, you must do it"?

   a. Pedro Martinez
   b. Al Leiter
   c. Nolan Ryan
   d. Tom Seaver

2. Which current Mets player once said: "I'm made in the Dominican. I'm from baseball country"?

   a. Wilson Ramos
   b. Robinson Cano
   c. Jeurys Familia
   d. Amed Rosario

3. Which former Met is quoted as saying: "I was a last-round draft pick. Nobody wanted me. I could count the

amount of scouts that told me to go to school, to forget baseball"?

   a. Darryl Strawberry

   b. Tom Seaver

   c. Mike Piazza

   d. Dwight Gooden

4. Which former Met once said: "When I look in the mirror, I look at the enemy. There is no one to blame for this but myself. I should have bought myself a mirror a long time ago"?

   a. Dwight Gooden

   b. Darryl Strawberry

   c. Jose Reyes

   d. Carlos Beltran

5. Which Met is quoted as saying: "One of the nicest satisfactions you can have is to be able to give something back to your parents when they've given so much to you"?

   a. Dwight Gooden

   b. Mike Piazza

   c. Pete Alonso

   d. David Wright

6. Which former Met is quoted as saying: "As soon as baseball becomes a job, as soon as I stop caring, as soon as the smile goes away, I'll hang up my spikes and do something else"?

a. Rickey Henderson

b. Nolan Ryan

c. Mike Piazza

d. David Wright

7. Which former Met is quoted as saying: "It's a grueling position. My knees will tell you that. I've had nine knee surgeries. I've had a couple of broken thumbs, one on each hand. I can look back at it and say it's worth it to be enshrined in Cooperstown. I don't have any pain in my knees right now"?

a. Mike Piazza

b. Tom Seaver

c. Gary Carter

d. Nolan Ryan

8. Former Met Darryl Strawberry once said, "A life is not important except in the impact it has on other lives."

a. True

b. False

9. Which former Mets manager is quoted as saying: "The key to being a good manager is keeping the people who hate me away from those who are still undecided"?

a. Bobby Valentine

b. Casey Stengel

c. Terry Collins

d. Yogi Berra

10. Which former Mets manager is quoted as saying: "Competing at the highest level is not about winning. It's about preparation, courage, understanding and nurturing your people, and heart. Winning is the result"?

    a. Joe Torre

    b. Davey Johnson

    c. Art Howe

    d. Gil Hodges

11. Which former Mets pitcher is quoted as saying: "My ability to throw a baseball was a God-given gift and I am truly appreciative of that gift"?

    a. Tom Seaver

    b. Dwight Gooden

    c. Nolan Ryan

    d. Jerry Koosman

12. When talking about Fernando Tatis Jr., which current Met is quoted as saying: "He's pretty much like a coke bottle when you shake him up and let it go and put Mentos in it. He's just really exciting and explosive"?

    a. Pete Alonso

    b. Robinson Cano

    c. Todd Frazier

    d. Michael Wacha

13. Which former Mets player is quoted as saying: "I'm not here to make money. I'm here to make history"?

    a. Robin Ventura

    b. Lenny Dykstra

c. Ron Darling

d. Tug McGraw

14. Which former Met is quoted as saying: "I just want to taste what it's like to win in New York"?

    a. Carlos Beltran

    b. Johan Santana

    c. Jose Reyes

    d. David Wright

15. Which Mets pitcher is quoted as saying: "Really no reason to be nervous when you're prepared. That's my motto"?

    a. Noah Syndergaard

    b. Tom Seaver

    c. Jacob deGrom

    d. Al Leiter

16. Former Met Rickey Henderson once said, "Never allow the fear of striking out keep you from playing the game."

    a. True

    b. False

17. Which former Mets pitcher is quoted as saying: "The more I grew as a human being, the better I became at my craft"?

    a. Matt Harvey

    b. Dwight Gooden

    c. R.A. Dickey

    d. Nolan Ryan

18. Which former Met once said: "Everyone has someone they looked up to. Mine was Mickey Mantle. For Alex Rodriguez to idolize me coming up, that makes me feel very good"?

    a. Robin Ventura
    b. Keith Hernandez
    c. Mike Piazza
    d. Darryl Strawberry

19. Which former Mets pitcher once said: "I enjoy every bit of baseball I can get"?

    a. Bartolo Colon
    b. Tom Glavine
    c. Ron Darling
    d. Pedro Martinez

20. Former Met Willie Mays once said: "Maybe I was born to play ball. Maybe I truly was."

    a. True
    b. False

QUIZ ANSWERS

1. D – Tom Seaver

2. B – Robinson Cano

3. C – Mike Piazza

4. B – Darryl Strawberry

5. A – Dwight Gooden

6. D – David Wright

7. C – Gary Carter

8. B – False (Jackie Robinson)

9. B – Casey Stengel

10. A – Joe Torre

11. C – Nolan Ryan

12. A – Pete Alonso

13. B – Lenny Dykstra

14. D – David Wright

15. A – Noah Syndergaard

16. B – False, Babe Ruth

17. C – R.A. Dickey

18. B – Keith Hernandez

19. D – Pedro Martinez

20. A – True

DID YOU KNOW?

1. Former Mets player and manager Yogi Berra was famous for his "Yogi-isms." He said the funniest things that usually either didn't quite make sense or were super-sarcastic. He was an amazing player and coach, but he is known for many of his quotes as well. Some examples: "Pair up in threes. " "It's déjà vu all over again." "You should always go to other people's funerals, otherwise they won't come to yours." "You can observe a lot by watching." "You better cut the pizza in four slices because I'm not hungry enough to eat six." "If you can't imitate him, copy him." "When you come to a fork in the road, take it." "Baseball is 90% mental and the other half is physical." "If the world were perfect, it wouldn't be."

2. "Here I am, a baseball superstar, falling into the pits, having everybody write you off, and then having God say, 'I'm going to use your mess for a message.' How beautiful is that?" – Darryl Strawberry

3. "When I went back to Shea last year, it really hit me how much the fans care for me; it still gives me goosebumps. I want to do the right thing for them and my family." – Dwight Gooden

4. "God is living in New York and he's a Mets fan." – Tom Seaver

5. "I love being a Met. It was my favorite team growing up,

so to be a Met, to me, is very special." – David Wright

6. "I did not want to leave the Mets and I did not leave New York." – Al Leiter

7. "It helps if the hitter thinks you're a little crazy." – Nolan Ryan

8. "My dream was to play football for the Oakland Raiders. But my mother thought I would get hurt playing football, so she chose baseball for me. I guess moms do know best." – Rickey Henderson

9. "I think I was the best baseball player I ever saw." – Willie Mays

10. "Sept. 11, 2001, is a day that forever changed our lives. To witness the darkest evil of the human heart and how it tore many loved ones from their families will forever be burned in my soul. But from tragedy and sorrow came bravery, love, compassion, character and, eventually, healing. Many of you give me praise for the two-run home run on the first game back on Sept. 21 to push us ahead of the rival Braves. But the true praise belongs to police, firefighters, first responders, who knew they were going to die, but went forward anyway. Jesus said there's no greater love than to lay down his life for his friends. I consider it a privilege to have witnessed that love. Your families and those left behind are always in my prayers. I pray we never forget their sacrifice and work to always defeat such evil." – Mike Piazza in his National Baseball Hall of Fame Speech in 2016

CHAPTER 4:

CATCHY NICKNAMES

QUIZ TIME!

1. Which nickname did pitcher Tom Seaver go by?

    a. Tom Terrific
    b. The Franchise
    c. Leave it to Seaver
    d. Both A & B

2. Lee Mazzilli's nickname was "The Italian Stallion."

    a. True
    b. False

3. What was Rusty Staub's nickname?

    a. Orange Rust
    b. Stauby
    c. Le Grande Orange
    d. Rustaub

4. What nickname did Darryl Strawberry go by?

    a. Straw
    b. D-Straw

c. Smashberry

d. Feral Darryl

5. Which is NOT a nickname for the Mets as a team?

   a. The Loveable Losers

   b. The Amazin' Mets

   c. The Met Men

   d. The Metropolitans

6. Which nickname did Lenny Dykstra NOT go by?

   a. The Dude

   b. The Len Man

   c. Nails

   d. Dr. Dirt

7. Noah Syndergaard has the nickname "Iron Man."

   a. True

   b. False

8. Which bear nickname does Mets 1B Pete Alonso go by?

   a. Grizzly Bear

   b. Polar Bear

   c. Panda Bear

   d. Black Bear

9. What is the famous nickname of former Mets pitcher Dwight Gooden?

   a. D-Good

   b. Do Right Dwight

   c. So Gooden

   d. Doc

10. What nickname was given to Edgardo Alfonzo?

   a. Fonzie
   b. Eddie Money
   c. Ed-Alf
   d. Zo

11. What nickname did C Gary Carter go by?

   a. Cart
   b. Kid
   c. G-Cart
   d. Catchin' Carter

12. Dwight Gooden got the nickname "Doc" because he was a pediatrician during the baseball offseason.

   a. True
   b. False

13. What was pitcher Matt Harvey's nickname?

   a. Batman
   b. The Dark Knight
   c. Harv
   d. Matty

14. What was the nickname of first baseman Keith Hernandez?

   a. El Toro
   b. El Toletero
   c. Mex
   d. Cali

15. David Wright goes by the nickname "Captain America."

    a. True
    b. False

16. Former Mets pitcher Tug McGraw went by the nickname _____.

    a. TMG
    b. The Graw Man
    c. T-Graw
    d. Tugger

17. Former Mets shortstop Jose Reyes had the nickname "La Melaza," Spanish for "Sweetness."

    a. True
    b. False

18. What was the nickname of former Mets third baseman Robin Ventura?

    a. Vent
    b. Robbie
    c. Batman
    d. The Dark Knight

19. What nickname did P Nolan Ryan go by?

    a. The Life of Ryan
    b. The Ryan Express
    c. Rollin' Nolan
    d. Flyin' Ryan

20. Willie Mays was given the nickname "The Say Hey Kid."

    a. True

    b. False

QUIZ ANSWERS

1. D – Both A & B

2. A – True

3. C – Le Grande Orange

4. A – Straw

5. C – The Met Men

6. B – The Len Man

7. B – False, "Thor"

8. B – Polar Bear

9. D – Doc

10. A – Fonzie

11. B – Kid

12. B – False

13. B – The Dark Knight

14. C – Mex

15. A – True

16. D – Tugger

17. A – True

18. C – Batman

19. B – The Ryan Express

20. A – True

DID YOU KNOW?

1. R.A. Dickey's full name is Robert Allen Dickey.

2. Former Met Mookie Wilson's real name is William Hayward Wilson. He was given the nickname "Mookie" as a small child.

3. Former Mets pitcher Bartolo Colon went by the nickname "Big Sexy."

4. Former Mets pitcher Al Leiter's full name is Alois Terry Leiter.

5. Former Met Rickey Henderson was often referred to as "The Man of Steal."

6. Former Mets manager and player Yogi Berra's real name is Lawrence Peter Berra. He was given the name by Jack Maguire, who when at the movie theater with Berra, noticed that he looked like the yogi (a person who practices yoga) on the screen.

7. Current Met Todd Frazier has the nickname "The ToddFather."

8. Former Mets outfielder Curtis Granderson goes by the nickname, "The Grandy Man."

9. Current Mets catcher Wilson Ramos got the nickname "The Buffalo" when he was with the Washington Nationals.

10. Dwight Gooden led the MLB in strikeouts his first two seasons, which earned him the nickname, "Dr. K." Over time, "Dr. K" was eventually shortened to simply "Doc."

CHAPTER 5:

THE FRANCHISE

QUIZ TIME!

1. What was Tom Seaver's full name?

    a. Thomas George Seaver

    b. George Thomas Seaver

    c. Thomas Michael Seaver

    d. Michael Thomas Seaver

2. Tom Seaver played his entire 20-season MLB career with the New York Mets.

    a. True

    b. False

3. Where was Tom Seaver born?

    a. Newport, Rhode Island

    b. Seattle, Washington

    c. Fresno, California

    d. Portland, Oregon

4. When is Tom Seaver's birthday?

    a. October 31, 1946
    b. October 31, 1944
    c. November 17, 1946
    d. November 17, 1944

5. Tom Seaver was elected to the National Baseball Hall of Fame in 1992 with 98.84% of the vote.

    a. True
    b. False

6. Tom Seaver passed away on _____, 2020, in his sleep at 75 years old due to complications from COVID-19 and Lewy body dementia.

    a. June 31
    b. August 31
    c. September 12
    d. September 30

7. How many MLB All-Star Games was Tom Seaver named to?

    a. 6
    b. 8
    c. 12
    d. 14

8. Tom Seaver was a 3x Cy Young Award winner (1969, 1973, and 1975).

    a. True
    b. False

9. Tom Seaver was chosen in the 10th round of the 1965 MLB draft by the _____ but did not sign. He was then drafted again, in the 1st round, 20th overall, by the _____ in the 1966 MLB January draft, secondary phase.

    a. New York Mets, Chicago White Sox
    b. Chicago White Sox, New York Mets
    c. Atlanta Braves, Los Angeles Dodgers
    d. Los Angeles Dodgers, Atlanta Braves

10. How many times did Tom Seaver lead the National League in ERA?

    a. 2 times
    b. 3 times
    c. 5 times
    d. 8 times

11. How many World Series championships did Tom Seaver win?

    a. 0
    b. 1
    c. 2
    d. 4

12. Tom Seaver was named the 1969 World Series MVP.

    a. True
    b. False

13. What year was Tom Seaver named the National League Rookie of the Year?

a. 1967

b. b. 1968

c. c. 1969

d. d. 1970

14. How many times did Tom Seaver lead the National League in wins?

    a. 1 time

    b. 2 times

    c. 3 times

    d. 6 times

15. How many times did Tom Seaver lead the National League in strikeouts?

    a. 1 time

    b. 3 times

    c. 5 times

    d. 8 times

16. How many strikeouts did Tom Seaver record during his 20-season MLB career?

    a. 2, 740

    b. 2, 640

    c. 3, 740

    d. 3, 640

17. Tom Seaver collected 311 MLB wins.

    a. True

    b. False

18. What year was Tom Seaver's uniform number retired by the New York Mets?

    a. 1985
    b. 1988
    c. 1990
    d. 1993

19. Where did Tom Seaver attend college?

    a. Pepperdine University
    b. San Jose State University
    c. University of Southern California
    d. California State University, Fresno

20. Tom Seaver made his MLB debut against the Pittsburgh Pirates and played his final game in the MLB against the Toronto Blue Jays.

    a. True
    b. False

QUIZ ANSWERS

1. B – George Thomas Seaver

2. B – False, Mets, Cincinnati Reds, Chicago White Sox, Boston Red Sox

3. C – Fresno, California

4. D – November 17, 1944

5. A – True

6. B – August 31

7. C – 12

8. A – True

9. D – Los Angeles Dodgers, Atlanta Braves

10. B – 3 times (1970, 1971, and 1973)

11. B – 1 (1969 with the Mets)

12. B – False, Donn Clendenon

13. A – 1967

14. C – 3 times (1969, 1975, and 1981)

15. C – 5 times (1970, 1971, 1973, 1975, and 1976)

16. D – 3, 640

17. A – True

18. B – 1988

19. C – University of Southern California (USC)

20. A – True

DID YOU KNOW?

1. New York City changed the address of Citi Field to 41 Seaver Way in 2019.

2. Tom Seaver threw a no-hitter on June 16, 1978, against the St. Louis Cardinals.

3. Seaver joined the U.S. Marine Corps Reserve in 1962. He served in Twentynine Palms, California, through July of 1963. He then enrolled in college and served his eight-year part-time Marine commitment until it ended in 1970.

4. Seaver is a member of the New York Mets Hall of Fame and the Cincinnati Reds Hall of Fame. He is also a member of the Marine Corps Sports Hall of Fame. He and Mike Piazza are the only two MLB players to be enshrined in the National Baseball Hall of Fame with a Mets cap on their plaques.

5. The Mets retired Seaver's uniform on Tom Seaver Day in 1988. He was the first Mets player to receive this honor.

6. During the "Shea Goodbye" closing ceremony, Seaver threw the final pitch in the stadium's history to Mike Piazza. He then threw the first pitch in Citi Field's history to Piazza the following year.

7. Only Tom Seaver and Walter Johnson recorded 300 wins, 3,000 strikeouts, and an ERA under 3.00.

8. Tom Seaver's 16 Opening Day starts are an MLB record. No MLB pitcher has ever matched his record of striking out 10 consecutive batters. He also holds the record for most consecutive 200-strikeout seasons at 9. Tom Seaver hit 12 home runs in his career and had a career batting average of .154. Not bad for a pitcher.

9. NFL Quarterback Tom Brady was denied the trademark "Tom Terrific" in 2019. The United States Patent and Trademark Office said it "may falsely suggest a connection with Tom Seaver."

10. Tom Seaver and his wife Nancy started Seaver Family Vineyards in Calistoga, California.

CHAPTER 6:

STATISTICALLY SPEAKING

QUIZ TIME!

1. Darryl Strawberry holds the New York Mets franchise record for home runs. How many did he hit?

    a. 242
    b. 252
    c. 302
    d. 352

2. Pitcher Tom Seaver had the most wins in New York Mets franchise history with 198.

    a. True
    b. False

3. Which pitcher holds the New York Mets record for most shutouts thrown in a single season, with 8 in 1985?

    a. Jon Matlack
    b. Jerry Koosman
    c. Tom Seaver
    d. Dwight Gooden

4. Which New York Mets batter holds the single-season record for strikeouts with 183 in 2019?

    a. Todd Frazier

    b. Pete Alonso

    c. Robinson Cano

    d. Joe Panik

5. Which pitcher has the most strikeouts in franchise history with a whopping 2,541?

    a. Dwight Gooden

    b. Sid Fernandez

    c. Tom Seaver

    d. Jacob deGrom

6. Who has the most stolen bases in New York Mets franchise history with 408?

    a. David Wright

    b. Howard Johnson

    c. Jose Reyes

    d. Mookie Wilson

7. Jeurys Familia holds the record for most saves in Mets history with 276.

    a. True

    b. False

8. Who holds the New York Mets record for being intentionally walked with 108?

    a. Darryl Strawberry

    b. Mike Piazza

    c. David Wright

    d. Howard Johnson

9. Which player holds the New York Mets franchise record for home runs in a single season with 53?

    a. Carlos Delgado

    b. Mike Piazza

    c. Carlos Beltran

    d. Pete Alonso

10. Who holds the single-season New York Mets record for hits with 227?

    a. Jose Reyes

    b. Lance Johnson

    c. David Wright

    d. John Olerud

11. Who holds the single-season New York Mets record for double plays grounded into with 27?

    a. Eddie Murray

    b. Gary Carter

    c. Mike Piazza

    d. Joe Torre

12. David Wright holds the record for the most sacrifice flies in New York Mets history with 65.

    a. True

    b. False

13. Tom Seaver threw the most wild pitches in New York Mets franchise history with how many?

a. 64

b. 81

c. 120

d. 145

14. Lance Johnson holds the New York Mets single-season record for most triples. How many did he hit in his record 1996 season?

    a. 28

    b. 23

    c. 21

    d. 20

15. Which hitter has the most walks in New York Mets franchise history with 762?

    a. David Wright

    b. Darryl Strawberry

    c. Bud Harrelson

    d. Ed Kranepool

16. Which New York Mets hitter holds the all-time franchise record for best batting average at .315?

    a. Mike Piazza

    b. Keith Hernandez

    c. Daniel Murphy

    d. John Olerud

17. Jose Reyes holds the New York Mets record for most runs scored with 949.

    a. True

    b. False

18. David Wright has the most plate appearances in New York Mets franchise history with how many?

   a. 4,872

   b. 5,872

   c. 6,872

   d. 8,872

19. Which pitcher holds the New York Mets franchise record for most saves in a single season with 51?

   a. Billy Wagner

   b. John Franco

   c. Armando Benitez

   d. Jeurys Familia

20. Jerry Koosman holds the New York Mets franchise record for most losses with 137.

   a. True

   b. False

QUIZ ANSWERS

1. B – 252

2. A – True

3. D – Dwight Gooden

4. B – Pete Alonso

5. C – Tom Seaver

6. C – Jose Reyes

7. B – False, John Franco

8. A – Darryl Strawberry

9. D – Pete Alonso (2019)

10. B – Lance Johnson (1996)

11. C – Mike Piazza (1999)

12. A – True

13. B – 81

14. C – 21

15. A – David Wright

16. D – John Olerud

17. B – False, David Wright

18. C – 6,872

19. D – Jeurys Familia (2016)

20. A – True

DID YOU KNOW?

1. Tom Seaver threw the most innings in New York Mets franchise history with 3,045.2. Coming in second is Jerry Koosman, who threw 2,544.2 innings.

2. John Olerud had the best single-season batting average in New York Mets franchise history at .354 in 1998. Mike Piazza comes in the second spot with a batting average of .348 the same season.

3. Carlos Beltran holds the New York Mets franchise record for stolen base percentage with 86.21% success. Jose Reyes holds the New York Mets franchise record for stolen bases with 408 and the franchise record for the most times caught stealing with 102.

4. David Wright has the most extra-base hits in New York Mets franchise history with 658. Second on the list is Jose Reyes with 493.

5. Dave Kingman holds the New York Mets franchise record for at-bats per home run at 15.1. Essentially what this means is that during his time with New York, Kingman hit a home run about every 15-16 at-bats.

6. Jacob deGrom holds the New York Mets franchise record for strikeouts per 9 innings pitched at 10.373. This basically means that deGrom recorded about 10-11 strikeouts in every 9 innings pitched.

7. Pitcher Pedro Astacio holds the single-season Mets record for the most batters hit by pitches with 16 in 2002.

8. David Wright holds the franchise record for double plays grounded into with 152.

9. Tom Seaver holds the Mets single-season record for wins with 25 in 1969. Second on the list is Dwight Gooden with 24 in 1985.

10. Roger Craig and Jack Fisher are tied for the New York Mets record for the most losses pitched in a single season with 24 each. Craig lost 24 games in 1962 and Fisher lost 24 games in 1965. Craig is also third on the list with 22 losses in 1963.

CHAPTER 7:

THE TRADE MARKET

QUIZ TIME!

1. On May 22, 1998, the New York Mets traded OF Preston Wilson, LHP Ed Yarnall, and LHP Geoff Goetz to the Florida Marlins for which player?

   a. Al Leiter
   b. Carlos Delgado
   c. Moises Alou
   d. Mike Piazza

2. On June 15, 1983, the New York Mets traded RHP Neil Allen and RHP Rick Ownbey to the St. Louis Cardinals for which player?

   a. Carlos Beltran
   b. Keith Hernandez
   c. Ken Boyer
   d. Fernando Tatis

3. The New York Mets have NEVER made a trade with the New York Yankees.

a. True

b. False

4. On December 10, 1984, the New York Mets traded OF/IF Hubie Brooks, C Mike Fitzgerald, OF Herm Winningham, and RHP Floyd Youmans to the Montreal Expos for who?

   a. Moises Alou

   b. Ron Darling

   c. Gary Carter

   d. Tim Foli

5. The New York Mets have only made six trades with the Tampa Bay Rays (as of the end of the 2020 season).

   a. True

   b. False

6. What year did the New York Mets trade Tom Seaver to the Cincinnati Reds?

   a. 1975

   b. 1976

   c. 1977

   d. 1978

7. On December 17, 2012, the New York Mets traded RHP R.A. Dickey, C Josh Thole, and C Mike Nickeas to the Toronto Blue Jays for C Travis d'Arnaud, C John Buck, Of Wuilmer Becerra, and which player?

   a. Noah Syndergaard

   b. Jose Bautista

    c. Curtis Granderson

    d. Rod Barajas

8. Which team traded OF Yoenis Cespedes to the New York Mets on July 31, 2015?

    a. Oakland A's

    b. Detroit Tigers

    c. Boston Red Sox

    d. Miami Marlins

9. The New York Mets traded OF Leroy Stanton, RHP Don Rose, C Frank Estrada, and which player to the California Angels for SS Jim Fregosi on December 10, 1971?

    a. Tim Foli

    b. Gil Flores

    c. Jack Hamilton

    d. Nolan Ryan

10. On February 2, 2008, the Mets traded OF Carlos Gomez, RHP Philip Humber, RHP Kevin Mulvey, and RHP Deolis Guerra to the Minnesota Twins for LHP Johan Santana.

    a. True

    b. False

11. On June 15, 1969, the Mets traded RHP Steve Renko, INF Kevin Collins, RHP Jay Carden, RHP David Colon, and 3B Terry Dailey to the Montreal Expos for who?

    a. Jim Gosger

    b. Duffy Dyer

c. Don Bosch

d. Donn Clendenon

12. The Mets have made only 11 trades with the Kansas City Royals (as of the end of the 2020 season) ever.

a. True

b. False

13. How many trades have the Mets made with the Oakland A's, as of the 2020 season?

a. 5

b. 10

c. 19

d. 20

14. The New York Mets NEVER traded Dwight Gooden.

a. True

b. False

15. On December 3, 2018, the Mets traded OF Jay Bruce, RHP Anthony Swarzak, RHP Gerson Bautista, OF Jarred Kelenic, and RHP Justin Dunn to which team for 2B Robinson Cano and RHP Edwin Diaz?

a. New York Yankees

b. Seattle Mariners

c. Los Angeles Dodgers

d. Miami Marlins

16. On April 6, 1972, the Mets traded Tim Foli, Ken Singleton, and Mike Jorgenson to the Montreal Expos for which player?

a. Don Hahn

b. Ray Burris

c. Rusty Staub

d. Ron Hunt

17. How many trades have the New York Mets made with the Los Angeles Dodgers (as of the 2020 season)?

a. 5

b. 10

c. 20

d. 25

18. On May 11, 1972, the Mets traded Charlie Williams to the San Francisco Giants for which player?

a. Willie Mays

b. Ray Sadecki

c. Bob Shaw

d. Mike Vail

19. On April 1, 1982, the New York Mets traded Lee Mazzilli to which team, for Ron Darling and Walt Terrell?

a. Oakland Athletics

b. Montreal Expos

c. Toronto Blue Jays

d. Texas Rangers

20. Five years after trading Tom Seaver to the Cincinnati Reds, the New York Mets re-acquired him from the Reds for Jason Felice, Lloyd McClendon, and Charlie Puleo.

a. True

b. False

QUIZ ANSWERS

1. D – Mike Piazza

2. B – Keith Hernandez

3. B – False, 14 trades as of the end of the 2020 season

4. C – Gary Carter

5. A – True

6. C – 1977

7. A – Noah Syndergaard

8. B – Detroit Tigers

9. D – Nolan Ryan

10. A – True

11. D – Donn Clendenon

12. A – True

13. C – 19

14. A – True (In fact, he was NEVER traded in his career.)

15. B – Seattle Mariners

16. C – Rusty Staub

17. D – 25

18. A – Willie Mays

19. D – Texas Rangers

20. A – True

DID YOU KNOW?

1. On December 7, 2011, the New York Mets traded OF Angel Pagan to the San Francisco Giants for Andres Torres and Ramon Ramirez.

2. On February 6, 1998, the Mets traded A.J. Burnett, Jesus Sanchez, and Rob Stratton to the Florida Marlins for Al Leiter and Ralph Milliard.

3. At the trade deadline in 1989, the Mets traded Mookie Wilson to the Toronto Blue Jays for Jeff Musselman and Mike Brady.

4. On June 18, 1989, the New York Mets traded Lenny Dykstra, a player to be named later (Tom Edens), and Roger McDowell to the Philadelphia Phillies for Juan Samuel.

5. On August 27, 1992, the New York Mets traded David Cone to the Toronto Blue Jays for Jeff Kent and a player to be named later (Ryan Thompson).

6. At the trade deadline in 1999, the New York Mets traded Jason Isringhausen and Greg McMichael to the Oakland A's for Billy Taylor.

7. On November 24, 2005, the New York Mets traded Yusmeiro Petit, Mike Jacobs, and Grant Psomas to the Florida Marlins for Carlos Delgado and cash.

8. On December 8, 1978, the New York Mets traded Jerry

Koosman to the Minnesota Twins for a player to be
named later (Jesse Orosco) and Greg Field.

9. On December 3, 1969, the New York Mets traded Amos
    Otis and Bob Johnson to the Kansas City Royals for Joe
    Foy.

10. On December 7, 2001, the New York Mets traded Robin
    Ventura to the New York Yankees for David Justice.

CHAPTER 8:

DRAFT DAY

QUIZ TIME!

1. Which MLB team drafted former Met, Mike Piazza in the 62nd round of the 1988 MLB draft?

    a. Oakland Athletics

    b. Los Angeles Dodgers

    c. Florida Marlins

    d. San Diego Padres

2. With the 1st overall pick in the first round of the 1980 MLB draft, the New York Mets selected which player?

    a. Billy Beane

    b. Wally Backman

    c. Dwight Gooden

    d. Darryl Strawberry

3. The New York Mets selected OF Hubie Brooks in the first round of the 2001 MLB draft, 3rd overall, from which college?

    a. San Diego State University

b. Arizona State University

c. Florida State University

d. Sacramento State University

4. With which overall pick, in the first round of the 1982 MLB draft, did the New York Mets select RHP Dwight Gooden?

    a. 1st

    b. 3rd

    c. 5th

    d. 11th

5. With the 14th overall pick in the first round of the 1973 MLB draft, the New York Mets selected which player?

    a. Lee Mazzilli

    b. Rich Puig

    c. Wally Backman

    d. John Gibbons

6. With the 38th overall pick in the first round of the 2001 MLB draft, the New York Mets selected which player?

    a. Aaron Heilman

    b. Scott Kazmir

    c. David Wright

    d. Philip Humber

7. Pete Alonso was drafted by the New York Mets in the first round of the 2016 MLB draft.

    a. True

    b. False

8. OF Curtis Granderson was drafted in the 3rd round of the 2002 MLB draft by which team?

    a. New York Yankees
    b. Detroit Tigers
    c. Los Angeles Dodgers
    d. Florida Marlins

9. With which overall pick in the first round of the 1968 MLB draft, did the New York Mets select SS Tim Foli?

    a. 1st
    b. 2nd
    c. 5th
    d. 8th

10. C Gary Carter was drafted by the Montreal Expos in the 3rd round of the 1972 MLB draft.

    a. True
    b. False

11. In the 42nd round of the 1971 MLB draft, which team selected 1B Keith Hernandez?

    a. Cleveland Indians
    b. New York Mets
    c. St. Louis Cardinals
    d. None of the Above

12. Al Leiter was drafted by the New York Mets in the 2nd round of the 1984 MLB draft.

a. True

b. False

13. In the first round of the 1981 MLB draft, which team selected RHP Ron Darling, 9th overall?

   a. Oakland Athletics

   b. New York Mets

   c. Minnesota Twins

   d. Texas Rangers

14. The New York Mets selected OF Michael Conforto 10th overall in the first round of which MLB draft, from Oregon State University?

   a. 2013

   b. 2014

   c. 2015

   d. 2016

15. Mookie Wilson was drafted by the New York Mets in which round of the 1977 MLB draft out of the University of South Carolina?

   a. 1st

   b. 2nd

   c. 4th

   d. 9th

16. LHP Sid Fernandez was drafted in the 3rd round of the 1981 MLB draft by which team?

   a. Houston Astros

   b. Philadelphia Phillies

c. Baltimore Orioles

d. Los Angeles Dodgers

17. 3B Robin Ventura was drafted 10th overall in the first round of the 1988 MLB draft out of Oklahoma State University by which team?

a. New York Yankees

b. Los Angeles Dodgers

c. Chicago White Sox

d. Kansas City Royals

18. LHP Jon Niese was drafted by the Mets in which round of the 2005 MLB draft?

a. 3rd

b. 7th

c. 9th

d. 12th

19. RHP Noah Syndergaard was drafted in the first round, 38th overall, in the 2010 MLB draft by which team?

a. Los Angeles Angels of Anaheim

b. New York Mets

c. Toronto Blue Jays

d. Oakland A's

20. In the 9th round of the 2010 MLB draft, the New York Mets selected RHP Jacob deGrom out of Stetson University.

a. True

b. False

QUIZ ANSWERS

1. B – Los Angeles Dodgers

2. D – Darryl Strawberry

3. B – Arizona State University

4. C – 5th

5. A – Lee Mazzilli

6. C – David Wright

7. B – False (2nd Round)

8. B – Detroit Tigers

9. A – 1st

10. A – True

11. C – St. Louis Cardinals

12. B – False, New York Yankees

13. D – Texas Rangers

14. B – 2014

15. B – 2nd

16. D – Los Angeles Dodgers

17. C – Chicago White Sox

18. C – 7th

19. C – Toronto Blue Jays

20. A – True

DID YOU KNOW?

1. CF Lenny Dykstra was drafted out of high school by the New York Mets in the 13th round of the 1981 MLB draft.

2. Tom Seaver was drafted by the Los Angeles Dodgers in the 10th round of the 1965 MLB draft but he did not sign with them. He was then drafted again in the 1st round, 20th overall, in the 1966 MLB draft by the Atlanta Braves out of the University of Southern California.

3. RHP A.J. Burnett was drafted by the New York Mets in the 8th round of the 1995 MLB draft, though he never actually played for the Mets.

4. Former Mets RHP Zack Wheeler was drafted out of high school by the San Francisco Giants in the first round, 6th overall, of the 2009 MLB draft.

5. OF Carlos Beltran was drafted out of high school in Puerto Rico by the Kansas City Royals in the 2nd round of the 1995 MLB draft.

6. LHP Jon Matlack was drafted out of high school by the New York Mets in the first round, 4th overall, in the 1967 MLB draft.

7. OF Rickey Henderson was drafted out of high school by the Oakland A's in the 4th round of the 1976 MLB draft.

8. RHP David Cone was drafted out of high school by the Kansas City Royals in the 3rd round of the 1981 MLB draft.

9. LHP Tom Glavine was drafted out of high school by the Atlanta Braves in the 2nd round of the 1984 MLB draft.

10. Current Met Todd Frazier was originally drafted by the Colorado Rockies in the 37th round of the 2004 MLB draft out of high school but decided to go to college instead. Three years later, he was drafted by the Cincinnati Reds in the first round of the 2007 MLB draft out of Rutgers University, 34th overall.

CHAPTER 9:

ODDS & ENDS

QUIZ TIME!

1. As part of his endorsement deal, David Wright owns 0.5% of which drink company?

    a. Smart Water

    b. Gatorade

    c. Vitamin Water

    d. La Croix

2. Jose Reyes was the cover athlete for the video game Major League Baseball 2K8 by 2K Sports.

    a. True

    b. False

3. Ron Darling played himself in which baseball movie?

    a. Fever Pitch

    b. Moneyball

    c. The Rookie

    d. Mr. 3000

4. Willie Mays is one of 66 holders of a lifetime pass on which airline?

   a. American Airlines
   b. United Airlines
   c. Southwest Airlines
   d. Hawaiian Airlines

5. In 2001, Mookie Wilson and his family released a gospel album. What did they call it?

   a. "The Wilsons Sing Gospel>"
   b. "For God So Loved the World"
   c. "God Will Get You Through"
   d. "Don't Worry, the Lord Will Carry You Through"

6. Former Met Jeff Kent appeared on which TV reality show?

   a. Big Brother
   b. Survivor
   c. The Amazing Race
   d. American Ninja Warrior

7. When Pedro Martinez was a kid, he could not afford baseballs, so he improvised with oranges.

   a. True
   b. False

8. What is the name of the documentary film that followed R.A. Dickey's 2011 season?

   a. Comeback
   b. Pitcher

c. Knuckleball

d. R.A.

9. Former Mets pitcher Tom Glavine was drafted by which team in the 1984 NHL Entry draft?

   a. Edmonton Oilers

   b. Calgary Flames

   c. Los Angeles Kings

   d. Winnipeg Jets

10. In July 2006, Rusty Staub teamed up with Mascot Books to publish a children's book. What was it titled?

   a. Go Mets Go

   b. Hello, Mr. Met

   c. Mr. and Mrs. Met

   d. The Amazin' Mets

11. What is the name of Dwight Gooden's autobiography?

   a. Doc Gooden: An Autobiography

   b. Dwight Gooden: My Life in the Big Leagues and Beyond

   c. The Gooden Times

   d. Doc: A Memoir

12. Country singer Tim McGraw is the son of former Phillies pitcher, Tug McGraw.

   a. True

   b. False

13. Lenny Dykstra's son Cutter is in a relationship with which actress?

a. Dakota Johnson

b. Lea Michele

c. Anna Kendrick

d. Jamie Lynn Sigler

14. Darryl Strawberry and his older brother Michael were drafted the same year, 1980.

a. True

b. False

15. Cleon Jones and several other members of the 1969 World Series champion Mets team appeared in a 1999 episode of which TV sitcom?

a. The King of Queens

b. Everybody Loves Raymond

c. Friends

d. Home Improvement

16. John Olerud is the cousin of former MLB player/manager Dale Sveum.

a. True

b. False

17. Jacob deGrom was a fan of which MLB team when he was growing up?

a. Atlanta Braves

b. New York Yankees

c. Tampa Bay Rays

d. Florida Marlins

18. Todd Frazier was a fan of which MLB team when he was growing up?

    a. New York Mets
    b. New York Yankees
    c. Cincinnati Reds
    d. Milwaukee Brewers

19. Bravo TV host Andy Cohen named his dog after which Mets pitcher?

    a. Matt Harvey
    b. Zack Wheeler
    c. Noah Syndergaard
    d. Michael Wacha

20. A species of weevil, *Sicoderus bautistai*, was named after Jose Bautista in 2018.

    a. True
    b. False

QUIZ ANSWERS

1. C – Vitamin Water

2. A – True

3. D – Mr. 3000

4. A – American Airlines

5. D – "Don't Worry, the Lord Will Carry You Through"

6. B – Survivor

7. A – True

8. C – Knuckleball

9. C – Los Angeles Kings

10. B – Hello, Mr. Met

11. D – Doc: A Memoir

12. A – True

13. D – Jamie Lynn Sigler

14. A – True

15. B – Everybody Loves Raymond

16. A – True

17. A – Atlanta Braves

18. B – New York Yankees

19. D – Michael Wacha

20. A – True

DID YOU KNOW?

1. The New York Mets will be paying Bobby Bonilla over $1 million every July 1 until 2035. By the end of the deal, Bonilla will have been paid $29.8 million for a season in which he did not even play for the Mets. Many Mets and baseball fans refer to July 1 as "Bobby Bonilla Day."

2. Pete Alonso competed for Florida in the 2015 and 2016 College World Series.

3. Al Leiter's brother Mark played in MLB for 11 seasons. He played for the New York Yankees, Detroit Tigers, California Angels, San Francisco Giants, Montreal Expos, Philadelphia Phillies, Seattle Mariners, and Milwaukee Brewers. Al's nephew, Mark Leiter Jr. played in the MLB as well.

4. The 11th edition of the Merriam-Webster Dictionary from 2012 credits Gary Carter with the first recorded use of the term "f-bomb."

5. The cartoon character Yogi Bear was similar enough to Yogi Berra's name that he considered suing Hanna-Barbera. The company claimed the similarity in name was simply a coincidence.

6. In a Season 1 episode of the TV sitcom, *Kevin Can Wait*, starring Mets fan Kevin James, Noah Syndergaard played a man wearing a Viking costume for Halloween.

7. Back in 2011, Mets catcher Wilson Ramos was kidnapped at gunpoint from his mother's house in Venezuela. He was taken on November 9 and rescued on November 12.

8. David Wright was chosen as the "Face of MLB" in an MLB Network online contest in 2014. He narrowly beat out Oakland A's infielder Eric Sogard.

9. During his career, Curtis Granderson wore high socks to honor players from the Negro Leagues.

10. In 2014, Mookie Wilson became an ordained Baptist minister.

CHAPTER 10:

OUTFIELDERS

QUIZ TIME!

1. Carlos Beltran played seven seasons with the New York Mets. Which of the following teams did he NOT play for during his 20-season career?

    a. Kansas City Royals
    b. St. Louis Cardinals
    c. Texas Rangers
    d. Miami Marlins

2. Former Mets centerfielder Angel Pagan did not win a World Series championship during his 11-season MLB career.

    a. True
    b. False

3. How many Silver Slugger Awards did former Mets outfielder Moises Alou win during his 17-year MLB career?

    a. 0

b. 2

c. 5

d. 10

4. Curtis Granderson was never named to an MLB All-Star Game in his 16-year MLB career.

   a. True

   b. False

5. Hubie Brooks played six seasons with the New York Mets. Which of the teams below did he NOT play for during his 15-season career?

   a. Montreal Expos

   b. Los Angeles Dodgers

   c. San Diego Padres

   d. California Angels

6. Former Mets centerfielder Willie Mays played for two teams in his 22-season MLB career, the Mets and which other team?

   a. New York/San Francisco Giants

   b. Brooklyn/Los Angeles Dodgers

   c. Boston Red Sox

   d. Chicago Cubs

7. Darryl Strawberry won the National League MVP Award in 1988.

   a. True

   b. False

8. How many seasons did outfielder Endy Chávez play for

the Mets?

    a. 1

    b. 2

    c. 3

    d. 4

9. How many stolen bases did left fielder Rickey Henderson accumulate during his two seasons with the New York Mets?

    a. 16

    b. 31

    c. 42

    d. 91

10. How many seasons did left fielder Jason Bay play for the New York Mets?

    a. 3

    b. 5

    c. 7

    d. 9

11. Center fielder Lenny Dykstra played for the New York Mets for five seasons. What was the one other team he played for during his MLB career?

    a. Philadelphia Phillies

    b. San Francisco Giants

    c. Toronto Blue Jays

    d. Atlanta Braves

12. Centerfielder Carlos Gomez started his MLB career as a

member of the New York Mets and also ended his MLB career as a member of the Mets.

a. True

b. False

13. How many home runs did Mets right fielder Michael Conforto hit during the 2020 season?

a. 13

b. 23

c. 33

d. 43

14. Darryl Strawberry won four World Series championships during his 17-season MLB career. How many of those championships did he win with the New York Mets?

a. 0

b. 1

c. 2

d. 3

15. How many MLB All-Star Games was center fielder Carlos Beltran named to during his 20-season MLB career?

a. 4

b. 6

c. 9

d. 13

16. Former Mets right fielder Jeff Francoeur played for eight different MLB teams during his 12-season career. Which of the teams below did he NOT play for?

a. Atlanta Braves

b. Los Angeles Angels of Anaheim

c. San Diego Padres

d. Kansas City Royals

17. How many times was former Mets left fielder Rickey Henderson named to the MLB All-Star Game during his 25-season career?

a. 10 times

b. 14 times

c. 17 times

d. 20 times

18. How many Gold Glove Awards did former Mets centerfielder Mike Cameron win during his 17-season MLB career?

a. 10

b. 9

c. 6

d. 3

19. Darryl Strawberry had back-to-back seasons with 39 home runs in which two years?

a. 1985-1986

b. 1986-1987

c. 1987-1988

d. 1988-1989

20. Former Mets outfielder Moises Alou is the half-brother of the current Mets' manager, Luis Rojas.

a. True
b. False

QUIZ ANSWERS

1. D – Miami Marlins

2. B – False, 2012 with the San Francisco Giants

3. B – 2

4. B – False, 3x All-Star

5. C – San Diego Padres

6. A – New York/San Francisco Giants

7. B – False (He came in 2nd behind Kirk Gibson.)

8. C – 3

9. C – 42

10. A – 3

11. A – Philadelphia Phillies

12. A – True

13. C – 33

14. B – 1

15. C – 9

16. B – Los Angeles Angels of Anaheim

17. A – 10 times

18. D – 3

19. C – 1987-1988

20. A – True

DID YOU KNOW?

1. Darryl Strawberry played 1,109 games for the New York Mets, the most of any team he played for during his 17-year MLB career. He also played for the New York Yankees, Los Angeles Dodgers, and San Francisco Giants.

2. Carlos Beltran played 839 games for the Mets, the most of any team he played for during his 20-year MLB career. He also played for the Kansas City Royals, New York Yankees, St. Louis Cardinals, Houston Astros, San Francisco Giants, and Texas Rangers.

3. Lee Mazzilli played 979 games for the New York Mets, the most of any team he played for during his 14-year MLB career. He won a World Series championship with the Mets in 1986 and was named to the All-Star Game. In addition to his 10 years with the Mets, he also played for the Pittsburgh Pirates, Texas Rangers, New York Yankees, and Toronto Blue Jays.

4. Angel Pagan played 393 games in four seasons for the New York Mets. He also played for the San Francisco Giants for five seasons and spent two seasons with the Chicago Cubs.

5. Lenny Dykstra played 544 games in five seasons with the Mets. He also played for the Philadelphia Phillies for eight seasons.

6. During his 25-season MLB career, Rickey Henderson was named MVP, a 10x All-Star, a Gold Glove Award winner, 2x Silver Slugger Award winner, ALCS MVP, and a 2x World Series champion. He was also named to the National Baseball Hall of Fame in 2009 as an Oakland A with 94.81% of the vote. He spent two seasons with the Mets and played in 152 games for them.

7. Moises Alou played 102 games in the two seasons he spent with the New York Mets. During his 17-year MLB career, he also played for the Montreal Expos, Chicago Cubs, Houston Astros, San Francisco Giants, Pittsburgh Pirates, and Florida Marlins.

8. Jeff Francoeur played 199 games in two seasons for the New York Mets. During his 12-season career, he also played for the Atlanta Braves, Kansas City Royals, Philadelphia Phillies, San Francisco Giants, Texas Rangers, San Diego Padres, and the Miami Marlins.

9. Hubie Brooks played 654 games in the six seasons he spent with the New York Mets, the most of any team he played for during his 15-year MLB career. He also played for the Montreal Expos, Kansas City Royals, Los Angeles Dodgers, and California Angels.

10. During his 22-season MLB career, Willie Mays was named a 2x MVP, Rookie of the Year, 24x All-Star, World Series champion, 12x Gold Glove Award winner, batting title winner, 2x All-Star MVP, and Major League Player of the Year. He was elected to the National

Baseball Hall of Fame in 1979 with 94.7% of the vote. He spent two seasons with the Mets and played in 135 games. He was named to his final All-Star Game in his final season in the MLB, with the Mets in 1973.

CHAPTER 11:

INFIELDERS

QUIZ TIME!

1. Former Mets infielder, Robin Ventura was manager of which MLB team from 2012 to 2016?

    a. Atlanta Braves
    b. Minnesota Twins
    c. Chicago White Sox
    d. Milwaukee Brewers

2. David Wright played his entire 14-season MLB career with the New York Mets.

    a. True
    b. False

3. How many stolen bases did former Mets infielder Jose Reyes record during his 12 seasons in New York?

    a. 375
    b. 399
    c. 408
    d. 459

4. Carlos Delgado played for the New York Mets for four seasons. He also played for the Florida Marlins and which other team?

    a. Philadelphia Phillies
    b. Toronto Blue Jays
    c. Los Angeles Dodgers
    d. Milwaukee Brewers

5. How many MLB All-Star Games was Daniel Murphy named to as a member of the New York Mets?

    a. 0
    b. 1
    c. 2
    d. 3

6. Mets second baseman Robinson Cano has played for which other two MLB teams besides the Mets (as of the 2020 season)?

    a. Houston Astros and Texas Rangers
    b. New York Yankees and Washington Nationals
    c. New York Yankees and Seattle Mariners
    d. Houston Astros and Seattle Mariners

7. In 2019, Mets first baseman Pete Alonso was named the National League Rookie of the Year, was an MLB All-Star, and won the MLB Home Run Derby.

    a. True
    b. False

8. Todd Frazier was a member of which Little League World Series championship team?

    a. 1995
    b. 1996
    c. 1997
    d. 1998

9. How many All-Star Games was David Wright named to in his 14-season career?

    a. 3
    b. 7
    c. 9
    d. 10

10. How many Gold Glove Awards did former Mets first baseman Keith Hernandez win during his 17-year MLB career?

    a. 2
    b. 8
    c. 11
    d. 15

11. How many times was former Mets shortstop Jose Reyes named an MLB All-Star in his 16-season MLB career?

    a. 1 time
    b. 2 times
    c. 4 times
    d. 7 times

12. Mets second baseman Robinson Cano was named after baseball legend Jackie Robinson.

    a. True
    b. False

13. What year did former Mets third baseman Edgardo Alfonzo win his sole Silver Slugger Award?

    a. 1998
    b. 1999
    c. 2000
    d. 2001

14. Fernando Tatis Jr., the son of former Mets third baseman Fernando Tatis, currently plays for which MLB team (as of the 2020 season)?

    a. Los Angeles Dodgers
    b. Washington Nationals
    c. Oakland A's
    d. San Diego Padres

15. How many games did third baseman Justin Turner play in during his four years with the Mets before signing with the Los Angeles Dodgers as a free agent?

    a. 301
    b. 311
    c. 321
    d. 351

16. David Wright was never named National League MVP.

    a. True
    b. False

17. What was second baseman Wally Backman's batting average for the Mets' 1986 world championship season?

    a. .310

    b. .320

    c. .330

    d. .340

18. How many Gold Glove Awards did Robin Ventura win during his 16-year MLB career?

    a. 1

    b. 3

    c. 5

    d. 6

19. How many home runs did Mets first baseman Pete Alonso hit in his rookie2020 season?

    a. 39

    b. 48

    c. 53

    d. 59

20. During his 14-season MLB career, David Wright won two Gold Glove Awards and two Silver Slugger Awards.

    a. True

    b. False

QUIZ ANSWERS

1. C – Chicago White Sox

2. A –True

3. C – 408

4. B – Toronto Blue Jays

5. B – 1 (2014)

6. C – New York Yankees and Seattle Mariners

7. A – True

8. D – 1998

9. B – 7

10. C – 11

11. C – 4 times (all with the Mets)

12. A – True

13. B – 1999

14. D – San Diego Padres

15. A – 301

16. A – True

17. B – .320

18. D – 6

19. C – 53

20. A –True

DID YOU KNOW?

1. Third baseman David Wright spent his entire 14-season career with the New York Mets. He is a 7x MLB All-Star, 2x Gold Glove Award winner, and a 2x Silver Slugger Award winner. He played 1,585 games, all with the Mets.

2. Shortstop Jose Reyes played for the New York Mets for 12 seasons. He also played for the Toronto Blue Jays, Colorado Rockies, and Miami Marlins. He is a 4x MLB All-Star, Silver Slugger Award winner, and batting title winner. He played 1,365 games with the Mets.

3. First baseman Keith Hernandez played for the New York Mets for seven seasons. He is a 5x MLB All-Star, MVP, 11x Gold Glove Award winner, 2x World Series champion, 2x Silver Slugger Award winner, and batting title winner. During his 17-year career, he also played for the St. Louis Cardinals and the Cleveland Indians. He played 880 games with the Mets and was a 1986 World Series champ.

4. Third baseman Robin Ventura played for the New York Mets for three seasons. He is a 2x MLB All-Star and a 6x Gold Glove Award winner. During his 16-year career, he also played for the Chicago White Sox, Los Angeles Dodgers, and New York Yankees. He was manager of the Chicago White Sox from 2012 to 2016. He played in 444 games with the Mets.

5. First baseman Carlos Delgado spent his final four seasons in the MLB with the Mets. He is a 2x MLB All-Star, 3x Silver Slugger Award winner, and winner of a Major League Player of the Year Award. He played in 468 games with the Mets.

6. Todd Frazier has been with the New York Mets for three seasons so far. As of the 2020 season, he is a 2x MLB All-Star. He won the 2015 Home Run Derby as a member of the Reds. He has also played for the Mets, Cincinnati Reds, Chicago White Sox, Texas Rangers, and New York Yankees.

7. Infielder Asdrubal Cabrera played for the New York Mets for three seasons. As of the 2020 season, he is a 2x MLB All-Star and Silver Slugger Award winner. He won the 2019 World Series championship with the Washington Nationals. He has played for the Mets, Nationals, Cleveland Indians, Texas Rangers, Tampa Bay Rays, and Philadelphia Phillies.

8. Third baseman Justin Turner played for the New York Mets for four seasons. As of the 2020 season, he is an MLB All-Star and NLCS MVP. He has played for the Mets and Baltimore Orioles but has spent the bulk of his time with the Los Angeles Dodgers. He played in 301 games with the Mets.

9. Second baseman Robinson Cano has played for the New York Mets for two seasons so far. As of the 2020 season, he is an 8x MLB All-Star, 2x Gold Glove Award winner,

5x Silver Slugger Award winner, All-Star MVP, and 2009 World Series champion. He has played for the Mets, New York Yankees, and Seattle Mariners.

10. Current Mets first baseman Pete Alonso has played for the New York Mets for only two seasons (so far). He was named the 2019 National League Rookie of the Year, won the 2019 Home Run Derby, and was a 2019 MLB All-Star. He hit a whopping 53 home runs in his rookie2020 season to lead the National League). The future looks bright for the Mets with Alonso on their side.

CHAPTER 12:

PITCHERS AND CATCHERS

QUIZ TIME!

1. Tom Seaver played for the New York Mets for 12 seasons. Which of the teams below did he NOT play for during his 20-year MLB career?

    a. Cincinnati Reds
    b. Chicago White Sox
    c. Oakland A's
    d. Boston Red Sox

2. Former Mets catcher Mike Piazza never won a World Series championship in his 16-year career.

    a. True
    b. False

3. How many All-Star Games was Dwight Gooden named to during his 16-year MLB career?

    a. 2
    b. 4
    c. 6

d. 8

4. How many World Series championships did Nolan Ryan win in his 27-year MLB career?

    a. 0
    b. 1
    c. 3
    d. 4

5. Catcher Yogi Berra played for and managed two teams during his 19-year MLB career. He played for and managed the Mets and which other team?

    a. Philadelphia Athletics
    b. New York Giants
    c. Brooklyn Dodgers
    d. New York Yankees

6. How many Cy Young Awards did former Mets pitcher Pedro Martinez win during his 18-year MLB career?

    a. 3
    b. 5
    c. 8
    d. 12

7. Former Mets pitcher Ron Darling was never named to an MLB All-Star Game.

    a. True
    b. False

8. How many All-Star Games was former Mets catcher Gary Carter named to during his 19-year MLB career?

a. 4

b. 9

c. 11

d. 16

9. Former Mets pitcher Matt Harvey was named National League Comeback Player of the Year in which year?

a. 2013

b. 2015

c. 2016

d. 2017

10. Mets pitcher Noah Syndergaard finished in what place in the 2015 National League Rookie of the Year voting?

a. 1st

b. 2nd

c. 3rd

d. 4th

11. Jeurys Familia has played for the New York Mets for nine seasons. To which team did the Mets trade him in 2018 before re-signing him as a free agent the following year?

a. Oakland A's

b. Kansas City Royals

c. Minnesota Twins

d. Atlanta Braves

12. Former Mets pitcher R.A. Dickey won his first Cy Young Award and was named to his first MLB All-Star Game

in 2012 as a member of the New York Mets, 11 years after he made his MLB debut.

    a. True

    b. False

13. How many Cy Young Awards did former Mets pitcher Johan Santana win during his 12-year MLB career?

    a. 0

    b. 1

    c. 2

    d. 5

14. How many All-Star Games was former Mets pitcher Al Leiter named to during his 19-season career?

    a. 2

    b. 4

    c. 8

    d. 12

15. What year was former Mets pitcher Tom Glavine inducted into the National Baseball Hall of Fame?

    a. 2012

    b. 2013

    c. 2014

    d. 2015

16. Former Mets pitcher Tug McGraw is the father of country music star Tim McGraw.

    a. True

    b. False

17. Pitcher Bartolo Colon was named to his final MLB All-Star Game as a member of the Mets in what year?

    a. 2015

    b. 2016

    c. 2017

    d. 2018

18. How many World Series championships did former Mets catcher Jerry Grote win during his 16-year MLB career?

    a. 0

    b. 1

    c. 2

    d. 4

19. Pitcher Dwight Gooden won a Silver Slugger Award as a member of the Mets in what year?

    a. 1990

    b. 1991

    c. 1992

    d. 1993

20. Former Mets pitchers Pedro Martinez, Al Leiter, and Ron Darling are all currently analysts on MLB Network.

    a. True

    b. False

QUIZ ANSWERS

1. C – Oakland A's

2. A – True

3. B – 4

4. B – 1 (1969 with the Mets)

5. D – New York Yankees

6. A – 3

7. B – False, 1x All-Star

8. C – 11

9. B – 2015

10. D – 4th (The Cubs' Kris Bryant won in 2015.)

11. A – Oakland A's

12. A – True

13. C – 2

14. A – 2

15. C – 2014

16. A – True

17. B – 2016

18. B – 1 (1969 with the Mets)

19. C – 1992

20. A – True

DID YOU KNOW?

1. Pitcher Tom Seaver played for the New York Mets for 12 seasons. During his 20-year MLB career, he also played for the Cincinnati Reds, Chicago White Sox, and the Boston Red Sox. He was named to the National Baseball Hall of Fame in 1992, is a 3x Cy Young Award winner, was named the 1967 National League Rookie of the Year, a 12x MLB All-Star, a 3x ERA Title winner, and a 1969 World Series champion with the Mets. His record with the Mets was 198-124.

2. Catcher Mike Piazza played for the New York Mets for eight seasons. During his 16-year MLB career, he also played for the Los Angeles Dodgers, Oakland A's, San Diego Padres, and Florida Marlins. He was named to the National Baseball Hall of Fame in 2016, was named the 1993 National League Rookie of the Year, is a 12x MLB All-Star, 10x Silver Slugger Award winner, and All-Star Game MVP. He played in 972 games with the Mets.

3. Pitcher Dwight Gooden played for the New York Mets for 11 seasons. During his 16-year MLB career, he also played for the New York Yankees, Cleveland Indians, Tampa Bay Devil Rays, and the Houston Astros. He is a Cy Young Award winner, was named the 1984 National League Rookie of the Year, won an NL Triple Crown in 1985, is a 4x MLB All-Star, a 2x World Series champion,

a Silver Slugger Award winner, and an ERA Title winner. He was a member of the Mets' 1986 World Series champion team. His record with the Mets was 157-85.

4. Pitcher Nolan Ryan played for the New York Mets for five seasons. During his 27-year MLB career, he also played for the Texas Rangers, Houston Astros, and California Angels. He was named to the National Baseball Hall of Fame in 1999 with 98.8% of the vote, is an 8x MLB All-Star, 2x ERA Title winner, and a 1969 World Series champion with the Mets. He never won a Cy Young Award. His record with the Mets was 29-38, the only losing record he had with any team he played for.

5. Catcher Yogi Berra only played for the Mets for one season. The other 18 years he spent playing in the majors was as a member of the New York Yankees. He only played in four games for the New York Mets at 40 years old but was their manager from 1972 to 1975. He was named to the National Baseball Hall of Fame in 1972, was a 3x MVP, an 18x MLB All-Star, and 10x World Series champion. Yes, 10. He truly loved New York.

6. Pitcher Pedro Martinez played for the New York Mets for four seasons. During his 18-year MLB career, he also played for the Boston Red Sox, Montreal Expos, Los Angeles Dodgers, and Philadelphia Phillies. He was named to the National Baseball Hall of Fame in 2015, is a 3x Cy Young Award winner, a 1999 American League

Triple Crown winner, an 8x MLB All-Star, a 5x ERA Title winner, All-Star Game MVP, and 2004 World Series champion. His record with the Mets was 32-23.

7. Catcher Gary Carter played for the New York Mets for five seasons. During his 19-year MLB career, he also played for the Montreal Expos, San Francisco Giants, and Los Angeles Dodgers. He was named to the National Baseball Hall of Fame in 2003, is an 11x MLB All-Star, 3x Gold Glove Award winner, 5x Silver Slugger Award winner, 2x All-Star Game MVP, and a 1986 World Series champion with the Mets. He played in a total of 600 games with the Mets.

8. Pitcher Al Leiter played for the New York Mets for seven seasons. During his 19-year MLB career, he also played for the Toronto Blue Jays, New York Yankees, and Florida Marlins. He is a 2x MLB All-Star and a 2x World Series champion. His record with the Mets was 95-67.

9. Pitcher Ron Darling played for the New York Mets for nine seasons. During his 13-year MLB career, he also played for the Oakland A's and the Montreal Expos. He is a 1x MLB All-Star, Gold Glove Award winner, and a 1986 World Series champion with the Mets. His record with the Mets was 99-70.

10. The New York Mets have had only one pitcher throw a no-hitter thrown. Johan Santana did it against the St. Louis Cardinals on June 1, 2012. You may be surprised

to hear that Tom Seaver and Doc Gooden never threw a no-hitter. Well, they did, just not with the Mets. In fact, several former Mets went on to pitch no-hitters/perfect games with other teams or had thrown them before they even became a Met. They include Tom Seaver, Dwight Gooden, Al Leiter, Don Cardwell, Kenny Rogers, Phil Humber, among others. There has never been a perfect game thrown in Mets franchise history.

CHAPTER 13:

WORLD SERIES

QUIZ TIME!

1. How many World Series have the New York Mets won in franchise history?

    a. 0

    b. 1

    c. 2

    d. 4

2. How many NL pennants have the Mets won?

    a. 3

    b. 5

    c. 7

    d. 9

3. Which team did the Mets face in the 1969 World Series?

    a. Baltimore Orioles

    b. Oakland Athletics

    c. Minnesota Twins

    d. Kansas City Royals

4. Which team did the New York Mets face in the 1986 World Series?

   a. Kansas City Royals
   b. Tampa Bay Rays
   c. Boston Red Sox
   d. Toronto Blue Jays

5. Who was the Mets' manager when they won the 1969 World Series?

   a. Yogi Berra
   b. Gil Hodges
   c. Joe Torre
   d. Casey Stengel

6. How many games did the 1969 World Series go?

   a. 4
   b. 5
   c. 6
   d. 7

7. Donn Clendenon was named the 1969 World Series MVP.

   a. True
   b. False

8. Which Mets player was named the 1986 World Series MVP?

   a. Gary Carter
   b. Darryl Strawberry
   c. Dwight Gooden
   d. Ray Knight

9. How many games did the 1986 World Series go?

    a. 4

    b. 5

    c. 6

    d. 7

10. Who was the Mets' manager when they won the 1986 World Series?

    a. Joe Torre

    b. Bobby Valentine

    c. Davey Johnson

    d. Terry Collins

11. Who did the Mets face in the 2000 World Series?

    a. Chicago White Sox

    b. Anaheim Angels

    c. Boston Red Sox

    d. New York Yankees

12. The New York Mets lost the 1973 World Series to the Oakland A's.

    a. True

    b. False

13. Which team did the Mets face in the 2015 World Series?

    a. Texas Rangers

    b. Kansas City Royals

    c. Houston Astros

    d. Detroit Tigers

14. Which of the following Mets did NOT hit a home run in the 1986 World Series?

    a. Gary Carter
    b. Darryl Strawberry
    c. Mookie Wilson
    d. Ray Knight

15. Which of the following Mets did NOT hit a home run in the 1969 World Series?

    a. Donn Clendenon
    b. Al Weis
    c. Ed Kranepool
    d. Cleon Jones

16. The New York Mets have never won a wild card berth.

    a. True
    b. False

17. Which team did the New York Mets beat in the 1969 NLCS to advance to the World Series?

    a. Los Angeles Dodgers
    b. Atlanta Braves
    c. Cincinnati Reds
    d. Houston Astros

18. Which team did the New York Mets beat in the 1986 NLCS to advance to the World Series?

    a. San Francisco Giants
    b. Houston Astros
    c. Florida Marlins
    d. Chicago Cubs

19. What was the final score of Game 5 of the 1969 World Series?

    a. Mets 5, Orioles 3

    b. Mets 6, Orioles 4

    c. Mets 10, Orioles 8

    d. Mets 2, Orioles 0

20. What was the final score of Game 7 of the 1986 World Series?

    a. Mets 9, Red Sox 6

    b. Mets 8, Red Sox 5

    c. Mets 4, Red Sox 1

    d. Mets 12, Red Sox 9

QUIZ ANSWERS

1. C – 2

2. B – 5

3. A – Baltimore Orioles

4. C – Boston Red Sox

5. B – Gil Hodges

6. B – 5

7. A – True

8. D – Ray Knight

9. D – 7

10. C – Davey Johnson

11. D – New York Yankees

12. A – True

13. B – Kansas City Royals

14. C – Mookie Wilson

15. D – Cleon Jones

16. B – False (3, in 1999, 2000, and 2016)

17. B – Atlanta Braves

18. B – Houston Astros

19. A – Mets 5, Orioles 3

20. B – Mets 8, Red Sox 5

DID YOU KNOW?

1. Tom Seaver and Jerry Koosman struck out the most Orioles hitters in the 1969 World Series with 9 strikeouts each. Ron Darling struck out the most Red Sox hitters in the 1986 World Series with 12 strikeouts.

2. Tommy Agee, Jerry Grote, Bud Harrelson, Cleon Jones, and Al Weis all played in all five games of the 1969 World Series. Gary Carter, Lenny Dykstra, Keith Hernandez, Rafael Santana, Mookie Wilson, and Darryl Strawberry all played in all seven games of the 1986 World Series.

3. Donn Clendenon had the best Mets batting average in the 1969 World Series at .357.

4. Jerry Koosman had the most wins during the 1969 World Series with 2. Rick Aguilera, Ron Darling, Roger McDowell, and Bob Ojeda each had 1 win in the 1986 World Series. No Mets pitcher had more than 1 win in the 1986 World Series.

5. The 1969 World Series took place from October 11 through October 16. The 1986 World Series took place from October 18 through October 27.

6. The Baltimore Orioles won Game 1 of the 1969 World Series. The Red Sox won Games 1, 2, and 5 of the 1986 World Series.

7. Game 1 of the 1969 World Series took place at Memorial Stadium in Baltimore. Commissioner Bowie Kuhn threw

out the first pitch and Joseph Eubanks sang the National Anthem.

8. Game 5 of the 1969 World Series was played at Shea Stadium in Queens. Joe DiMaggio threw out the first pitch and Pearl Bailey sang the National Anthem.

9. Game 1 of the 1986 World Series took place at Shea Stadium in Queens. National League President Chub Feeney threw out the first pitch and Glenn Close sang the National Anthem.

10. Game 7 of the 1986 World Series was played at Shea Stadium. New York Mets Owner Nelson Doubleday Jr. threw out the first pitch and Kenneth Mack sang the National Anthem.

CHAPTER 14:

HEATED RIVALRIES

QUIZ TIME!

1. Which team does NOT play in the National League East with the Mets?

    a. Miami Marlins

    b. Philadelphia Phillies

    c. Washington Nationals

    d. Baltimore Orioles

2. The Mets are a founding member of the NL East Division.

    a. True

    b. False

3. Which team did not move from the NL East to the NL Central in 1994?

    a. Chicago Cubs

    b. Pittsburgh Pirates

    c. Toronto Blue Jays

    d. St. Louis Cardinals

4. The New York Mets have two World Series championships. How many do the Philadelphia Phillies have?

    a. 0

    b. 2

    c. 4

    d. 5

5. The New York Mets have two World Series championships. How many do the Atlanta Braves have?

    a. 0

    b. 2

    c. 3

    d. 7

6. The New York Mets have won two World Series championships. How many have the New York Yankees won?

    a. 10

    b. 17

    c. 20

    d. 27

7. The Mets have the most NL East championships of any team in the division.

    a. True

    b. False

8. Which player has NOT played for both the Mets and the Phillies?

a. Tom Seaver

b. Bobby Abreu

c. Larry Bowa

d. Pedro Martinez

9. Which player has NOT played for both the Mets and the Yankees?

a. Robinson Cano

b. Bartolo Colon

c. Gary Carter

d. Curtis Granderson

10. Which player has NOT played for both the Mets and the Braves?

a. Sandy Alomar

b. Mike Piazza

c. Lucas Duda

d. Tom Glavine

11. Which player has NOT played for both the Mets and the Marlins?

a. Mike Piazza

b. Carlos Delgado

c. Ron Darling

d. Al Leiter

12. The New York Mets and New York Yankees have never faced each other in the World Series.

a. True

b. False

13. Which NL East team has NEVER won the NL East Division title?

    a. Philadelphia Phillies
    b. Florida/Miami Marlins
    c. Montreal Expos/Washington Nationals
    d. Atlanta Braves

14. The NL East is one of only two MLB divisions to have every team win at least one World Series championship. What is the other division?

    a. American League West
    b. American League East
    c. American League Central
    d. American League West

15. What is the name of the series between the New York Mets and New York Yankees?

    a. New York Series
    b. Bridge Series
    c. Subway Series
    d. Empire State Series

16. The Montreal Expos have won one National League East title, in 1981.

    a. True
    b. False

17. As of the end of the 2020 season, the last time the Mets won the division was 2015. When was the last time the Washington Nationals won the division?

a. 2012
b. 2014
c. 2017
d. 2019

18. As of the end of the 2020 season, the last time the Mets won the division was 2015. When was the last time the Atlanta Braves won the division?

    a. 2005
    b. 2013
    c. 2018
    d. 2019

19. As of the end of the 2020 season, the last time the Mets won the division was 2015. When was the last time the Philadelphia Phillies won the division?

    a. 1993
    b. 2008
    c. 2011
    d. 2013

20. The Mets, Phillies, and Expos/Nationals are the only founding members left in the NL East.

    a. True
    b. False

QUIZ ANSWERS

1. D – Baltimore Orioles

2. A – True

3. C – Toronto Blue Jays

4. B – 2

5. C – 3

6. D – 27

7. B – False (The Atlanta Braves have won 14; the Mets have 6.)

8. A – Tom Seaver

9. C – Gary Carter

10. B – Mike Piazza

11. C – Ron Darling

12. B – False (2000 World Series)

13. B – Florida/Miami Marlins

14. C – American League Central

15. C – Subway Series

16. A – True

17. C – 2017

18. D – 2019

19. C – 2011

20. A – True (Braves were in the NL West until 1994 and the Marlins are an expansion team that joined in 1993.)

DID YOU KNOW?

1. The Mets and Yankees used to play each other only in exhibition games until the introduction of interleague play. The two teams have played each other every regular season since 1997.

2. When the NL Central was created, the Braves were originally supposed to move and the Pirates were supposed to stay in the NL East. However, the Braves wanted to stay in a division with the Marlins. The Marlins offered to go to the NL Central but the Pirates ultimately were the ones to change divisions.

3. The 2000 World Series between the Mets and Yankees went 5 games, with the Yankees winning 4 games to the Mets 1. It was the Yankees' third consecutive World Series championship.

4. The rivalry between the Mets and Atlanta Braves rivalry truly began in the 1969 NLCS when the Mets swept the Braves on their way to their first World Series championship.

5. The Mets and Phillies rivalry resulted in several brawls in the 1980s. Between 2006 and 2008, it was ranked as one of the hottest rivalries in the National League.

6. The Atlanta Braves have won the NL East Division 14 times, the Philadelphia Phillies 11 times, the Pittsburgh Pirates 9 times, the New York Mets 6 times, the

Washington Nationals 5 times, the St. Louis Cardinals 3 times, and the Chicago Cubs 2 times. The Florida/Miami Marlins have never won the division.

7. Moises Alou, Rick Ankiel, Hubie Brooks, Marlon Byrd, Asdrubal Cabrera, Gary Carter, Endy Chavez, Donn Clendenon, Tyler Clippard, Bartolo Colon, Alex Cora, Ron Darling, Tim Foli, Pedro Martinez, Fernando Tatis, and Wilson Ramos have all played for both the Mets and the Expos/Nationals.

8. Bobby Abreu, Rod Barajas, Jose Bautista, Larry Bowa, Marlon Byrd, Asdrubal Cabrera, Don Cardwell, Lenny Dykstra, Jeff Francoeur, Tug McGraw, and Jason Vargas have all played for both the Mets and the Philadelphia Phillies.

9. Sandy Alomar, Jose Bautista, Jerry Blevins, Terry Blocker, Bobby Bonilla, Don Cardwell, Bartolo Colon, R.A. Dickey, Octavio Dotel, Lucas Duda, Jeff Francoeur, Tom Glavine, Billy Hamilton, Juan Uribe, and Gary Sheffield have all played for both the Mets and the Atlanta Braves.

10. Bobby Abreu, Sandy Alomar, Carlos Beltran, Yogi Berra, Dellin Betances, Robinson Cano, Tyler Clippard, Bartolo Colon, David Cone, Ike Davis, Octavio Dotel, Tony Fernandez, Tim Foli, Todd Frazier, Dwight Gooden, Curtis Granderson, LaTroy Hawkins, Rickey Henderson, Al Leiter, Lee Mazzilli, John Olerud, Willie Randolph, Kenny Rogers, Gary Sheffield, Darryl Strawberry, Robin Ventura, and Jose Vizcaino have all played for both the Mets and the New York Yankees.

CHAPTER 15:

THE AWARDS SECTION

QUIZ TIME!

1. Which New York Mets pitcher won the National League Cy Young Award in 2012?

    a. Johan Santana

    b. R.A. Dickey

    c. Matt Harvey

    d. Jon Niese

2. No New York Mets catcher has ever won a National League Gold Glove Award.

    a. True

    b. False

3. Which Mets player won a Silver Slugger Award in 2016?

    a. Jay Bruce

    b. Curtis Granderson

    c. Jose Reyes

    d. Yoenis Cespedes

4. Which Met most recently won the NL Rookie of the Year Award (as of the end of the 2020 season)?

    a. Darryl Strawberry
    b. Dwight Gooden
    c. Jacob deGrom
    d. Pete Alonso

5. Who is the only pitcher in New York Mets history to win a Rawlings Gold Glove Award?

    a. Jacob deGrom
    b. Tom Seaver
    c. Ron Darling
    d. Dwight Gooden

6. Which New York Mets pitcher won a Silver Slugger Award in 2000?

    a. Al Leiter
    b. Rick Reed
    c. Pat Mahomes
    d. Mike Hampton

7. No New York Mets manager has ever won a National League Manager of the Year Award.

    a. True
    b. False

8. Which Met was named the DHL Hometown Hero? (Voted by MLB fans as the most outstanding player in franchise history.)

    a. Dwight Gooden
    b. David Wright

    c. Tom Seaver

    d. Mike Piazza

9. Who was the first New York Mets player named National League Rookie of the Year?

    a. Tom Seaver

    b. John Matlack

    c. Darryl Strawberry

    d. Dwight Gooden

10. How many Silver Slugger Awards did Mike Piazza win with the New York Mets?

    a. 2

    b. 4

    c. 5

    d. 7

11. Which New York Mets pitcher was named the Wilson MLB Defensive Player of the Year in 2015?

    a. Matt Harvey

    b. Bartolo Colon

    c. Noah Syndergaard

    d. Jacob deGrom

12. No New York Mets player has ever won a Hank Aaron Award.

    a. True

    b. False

13. Who won a Major League/NL Pitching Triple Crown in 1985?

a. Ron Darling

b. Ed Lynch

c. Dwight Gooden

d. Sid Fernandez

14. Who was named the 1999 MLB Comeback Player of the Year?

a. Mike Piazza

b. Rickey Henderson

c. Bobby Bonilla

d. Al Leiter

15. Who is the only New York Mets executive ever to win Baseball America's Major League Executive of the Year Award?

a. Sandy Alderson

b. Frank Cashen

c. Paul DePodesta

d. Steve Phillips

16. No New York Mets player has ever WON the Home Run Derby.

a. True

b. False

17. Which Mets player won a Roberto Clemente Award in 2000?

a. Mike Piazza

b. Robin Ventura

c. Al Leiter

d. Jay Payton

18. Who is the only Mets second baseman ever to win an NL Gold Glove Award (as of the end of the 2020 season)?

    a. Doug Flynn
    b. Roberto Alomar
    c. Daniel Murphy
    d. Wally Backman

19. Who is the only New York Mets first baseman ever to win an NL Gold Glove Award during his time with the Mets (as of the end of the 2020 season)?

    a. Carlos Delgado
    b. Ike Davis
    c. Lucas Duda
    d. Keith Hernandez

20. Tom Seaver won the most Cy Young Awards in New York Mets history with 3.

    a. True
    b. False

QUIZ ANSWERS

1. B – R.A. Dickey

2. A – True

3. D – Yoenis Cespedes

4. D – Pete Alonso (2019)

5. C – Ron Darling

6. D – Mike Hampton

7. A – True

8. C – Tom Seaver

9. A – Tom Seaver (1967)

10. C – 5

11. D – Jacob deGrom

12. A – True

13. C – Dwight Gooden

14. B – Rickey Henderson

15. A – Sandy Alderson (2015)

16. B – False (Darryl Strawberry in 1986 and Pete Alonso in 2019)

17. C – Al Leiter

18. A – Doug Flynn (1980)

19. D – Keith Hernandez (1983-1988)

20. A – True

DID YOU KNOW?

1. The New York Mets have had four Cy Young Award winners in franchise history: Tom Seaver (1969, 1973, and 1975), Dwight Gooden (1985), R.A. Dickey (2012), and Jacob deGrom (2018, 2019).

2. Jose Reyes is the only shortstop in franchise history ever to win an NL Silver Slugger Award (2006).

3. Six New York Mets have been named NL Rookie of the Year: Tom Seaver (1967), John Matlack (1972), Darry Strawberry (1983), Dwight Gooden (1984), Jacob deGrom (2014), and Pete Alonso (2019).

4. The 2012 and 2013 New York Mets as a team were named the Wilson Defensive Players of the Year.

5. No Mets player has ever been named National League MVP (as of the end of the 2020 season).

6. Two New York Mets players have been given the Rolaids Relief Man of the Year Award in franchise history: John Franco (1990) and Armando Benitez (2001)

7. The only Mets player to win the All-Star Game MVP Award was John Matlack in 1975. He shared the honor with Bill Madlock of the Chicago Cubs.

8. Two New York Mets have been named NLCS MVP: Mike Hampton (2000) and Daniel Murphy (2015).

9. Two New York Mets have been named World Series MVP: Donn Clendenon (1969) and Ray Knight (1986).

10. The first Mets player to win a Gold Glove Award was outfielder Tommie Agee in 1970.

CHAPTER 16:

THE KINGS OF QUEENS

QUIZ TIME!

1. Queens is named after which queen?

    a. Queen Mary
    b. Queen Elizabeth
    c. Queen Catherine
    d. Queen Victoria

2. Magician Harry Houdini is buried in Queens.

    a. True
    b. False

3. If Queens were to secede from the rest of New York, how would it rank in population among U.S. cities?

    a. 2nd
    b. 4th
    c. 8th
    d. 11th

4. Which band got its start rehearsing in an art gallery on Queens Blvd?

    a. Pink Floyd
    b. Green Day
    c. The Ramones
    d. Nirvana

5. Which of the celebrities listed below is NOT from Queens?

    a. Ray Romano
    b. Tony Bennett
    c. LL Cool J
    d. Beyoncé

6. Queens is home to which airport?

    a. JFK International Airport
    b. LaGuardia Airport
    c. Newark International Airport
    d. Both A & B

7. The U.S. Open (tennis) takes place in Queens.

    a. True
    b. False

8. What is the name of the film festival that is held annually in Queens?

    a. Queens Film Festival
    b. Queens World Film Festival
    c. New York World Film Fest
    d. Film Festival Queens

9. What is the name of New York's NFL team?

   a. New York Dolphins
   b. New York Jets
   c. New York Giants
   d. Both B & C

10. What is the name of New York's NBA team?

   a. New York Knicks
   b. Brooklyn Nets
   c. New York Warriors
   d. Both A & B

11. What is the name of New York's NHL team?

   a. New York Rangers
   b. New York Islanders
   c. New York Flyers
   d. Both A & B

12. Stockholm Street in Ridgewood is the only brick road in Queens.

   a. True
   b. False

13. Queens is known as the capital of what in New York City?

   a. Art
   b. Beer
   c. Cemetery
   d. Music

14. Queens is the birthplace of which popular board game?

    a. Clue
    b. Monopoly
    c. Chutes and Ladders
    d. Scrabble

15. Which studio in Queens is home to New York City's only movie backlot?

    a. Silvercup Studios
    b. Kaufman Astoria Studios
    c. NBC Studios
    d. Screen Gem Studios

16. Queens is the largest of the five boroughs in New York.

    a. True
    b. False

17. Kaufman Astoria Studios in Queens is the home of which popular children's TV program?

    a. Reading Rainbow
    b. Mr. Rogers' Neighborhood
    c. Sesame Street
    d. Barney and Friends

18. Which Queens racetrack is the only one located within New York City Limits?

    a. Aqueduct Racetrack
    b. Yonkers Raceway
    c. Floyd Bennett Field Raceway
    d. Belmont Park

19. According to the 2010 census, what percentage of all Queens households did not own a car?

    a. 16%

    b. 36%

    c. 56%

    d. 86%

20. The world's first road made specifically for cars was paved in Queens. It is now a bike path.

    a. True

    b. False

QUIZ ANSWERS

1. C – Queen Catherine

2. A – True

3. B – 4th

4. C – The Ramones

5. D – Beyoncé

6. D – Both A & B

7. A –True

8. B – Queens World Film Festival

9. D – Both B & C

10. D –Both A & B

11. D – Both A & B

12. A – True

13. C – Cemetery

14. D – Scrabble

15. B – Kaufman Astoria Studios

16. A – True

17. C – Sesame Street

18. A – Aqueduct Racetrack

19. B – 36%

20. A – True

DID YOU KNOW?

1. *The King of Queens* sitcom, starring Kevin James, Leah Remini, and Jerry Stiller, ran from 1998-2007 for nine seasons. The show focused on a couple living in Queens. The main character, Doug Heffernan (played by James) was a huge Mets fan.

2. Queens Botanical Garden, in Flushing, evolved from an exhibit showcased at the 1939-1940 World's Fair. Today it is a 39-acre piece of land owned by the City of New York, open to all visitors.

3. Queens was essential to the 1940s jazz scene. For example, Louis Armstrong and Ella Fitzgerald moved to Queens to escape harsh segregation. In Corona, you can take a tour of the Louis Armstrong House Museum where he spent 30 years of his life.

4. The New York Hall of Science, located in Queens, was founded at the 1964-1965 World's Fair. It is now the center for interactive science in the area.

5. Queens uses hyphenated addresses. For example, 53-51 111th St. Corona, NY 11368 (Queens Zoo)

6. Queens Zoo was constructed on the site of the 1964 World's Fair. It opened in 1968 as the first zoo designed from the start to be cageless. When it opened, it was named the "Flushing Meadows Zoo." It is 18 acres big

and houses over 75 species that are native to the Americas. It is the only zoo in NYC that Andean bears call home.

7. Spiderman (Peter Parker) was born in Queens, was where he grew up, and where he ultimately became Spiderman.

8. Forest Hills Stadium was constructed in Queens in 1923 on open farmland. It was the original home of the U.S. Open and the Davis Cup. In the 1960s, music concerts took over. Forest Hills has hosted the likes of The Beatles, Frank Sinatra, The Supremes, Bob Dylan, Judy Garland, Jimi Hendrix, The Who, and Donna Summer. It was also featured in the Alfred Hitchcock film, *Strangers on a Train* and Wes Anderson's *The Royal Tenenbaums*.

9. Queens is one of the most ethnically diverse countries in the United States. It is also the most linguistically diverse place in the world.

10. LaGuardia Airport's code is "LGA." JFK Airport's code is obviously "JFK." It was originally opened as the New York International Airport, but its name was changed after John F. Kennedy's assassination to honor the fallen 35th President.

CHAPTER 17:

PIAZZA

QUIZ TIME!

1. Where was Mike Piazza born?

    a. San Diego, California

    b. Norristown, Pennsylvania

    c. Venice, Italy

    d. Fernley, Nevada

2. Mike Piazza's full name is Michael Joseph Piazza.

    a. True

    b. False

3. Mike Piazza played for the New York Mets for 8 of the 16 seasons he spent in the major leagues. He also played for the Los Angeles Dodgers, Florida Marlins, San Diego Padres, and which other team?

    a. New York Yankees

    b. Philadelphia Phillies

    c. Washington Nationals

    d. Oakland A's

4. What year was Mike Piazza born?

    a. 1967
    b. 1968
    c. 1969
    d. 1970

5. What year was Mike Piazza's No. 31 retired by the Mets?

    a. 2012
    b. 2014
    c. 2016
    d. 2018

6. How many Silver Slugger Awards (consecutively!) did Mike Piazza win during his 16-season MLB career?

    a. 3
    b. 6
    c. 8
    d. 10

7. Mike Piazza was named the 1993 National League Rookie of the Year.

    a. True
    b. False

8. How many MLB All-Star Games was Mike Piazza named to?

    a. 9
    b. 10
    c. 12
    d. 13

9. Which college was Mike Piazza drafted out of by the Los Angeles Dodgers?

   a. Florida State University
   b. Miami Dade College
   c. University of Florida
   d. University of Miami

10. What year was Mike Piazza named the MLB All-Star Game MVP?

   a. 1995
   b. 1996
   c. 1999
   d. 2001

11. How many Gold Glove Awards did Mike Piazza win during his 16-season MLB career?

   a. 9
   b. 3
   c. 1
   d. 0

12. Tommy Lasorda is the godfather of Mike Piazza's youngest brother, Tommy.

   a. True
   b. False

13. What year was Mike Piazza inducted into the National Baseball Hall of Fame with 82.95% of the vote?

   a. 2012
   b. 2014

c. 2016

d. 2018

14. Mike Piazza made his MLB debut against which team, and played the final game of his career against which team?

    a. Seattle Mariners, San Francisco Giants

    b. San Francisco Giants, Seattle Mariners

    c. California Angels, Chicago Cubs

    d. Chicago Cubs, Los Angeles Angels of Anaheim

15. In what year did Mike Piazza win the ESPN ESPY Award for Breakthrough Athlete?

    a. 1992

    b. 1994

    c. 1996

    d. 1998

16. Mike Piazza received personal instruction from Ted Williams in his backyard batting cage. Williams told Piazza to not let anyone tell him to change his swing, told him he had talent, and gave him an autographed copy of his book, *The Science of Hitting*.

    a. True

    b. False

17. How many home runs did Mike Piazza hit in his 16-year MLB career?

    a. 399

    b. 418

c. 427

d. 527

18. What is Mike Piazza's career batting average?

    a. .299

    b. .308

    c. .318

    d. .328

19. How many home runs did Mike Piazza hit as a member of the New York Mets?

    a. 200

    b. 210

    c. 220

    d. 240

20. Mike Piazza's father Vince tried several times to purchase an MLB franchise when Mike was still a kid.

    a. True

    b. False

QUIZ ANSWERS

1. B – Norristown, Pennsylvania

2. A – True

3. D – Oakland A's

4. B – 1968

5. C – 2016

6. D – 10

7. A – True

8. C – 12

9. B – Miami Dade College

10. B – 1996

11. D – 0

12. A – True

13. C – 2016

14. D – Chicago Cubs, Los Angeles Angels of Anaheim

15. B – 1994

16. A – True

17. C – 427

18. B – .308

19. C – 220

20. A – True

DID YOU KNOW?

1. On September 21, 2001, 10 days after the deadly 9/11 terrorist attacks in New York City, Mike Piazza hit a home run in the first professional sporting event in New York since the attacks.

2. Mike Piazza owns the Italian soccer team A.C. Reggiana 1919.

3. Piazza was originally drafted by the Los Angeles Dodgers as a favor from Tommy Lasorda to Piazza's father, Vince who was a childhood friend of Lasorda's.

4. Mike Piazza represented Italy in the 2006 World Baseball Classic, he was Italy's hitting coach in the 2009 and 2013 World Baseball Classics, and he has announced that he will manage Italy's team in the 2021 World Baseball Classic.

5. Mike Piazza released an autobiography in 2013 entitled *Long Shot*.

6. Mike Piazza appeared in the movie *Two Weeks Notice* and on the TV show *Married with Children*.

7. Mike Piazza, Derek Jeter, and Bernie Williams are the only players in MLB history to hit World Series home runs in both Shea Stadium and Yankee Stadium.

8. Mike Piazza led All-Star voting in 1996, 1997, and 2000.

9. "[Piazza is a] first-ballot Hall of Famer, certainly the best hitting catcher of our era and arguably the best hitting catcher of all time." – Tom Glavine

10. Mike Piazza hit over 30 home runs in eight consecutive seasons (1995-2002) and he had nine career 30-home run seasons.

CHAPTER 18:

STRAW

QUIZ TIME!

1. Where was Darryl Strawberry born?

    a. Fort Wayne, Texas

    b. Dallas, Texas

    c. Los Angeles, California

    d. Oakland, California

2. Darry Strawberry is a member of the New York Mets Hall of Fame.

    a. True

    b. False

3. Jimmy Rollins played for four MLB teams during his 17-season MLB career; the Mets, the Los Angeles Dodgers, the San Francisco Giants, and which other team?

    a. Chicago Cubs

    b. St. Louis Cardinals

    c. New York Yankees

    d. Oakland Athletics

4. What year was Darryl Strawberry born?

    a. 1960
    b. 1962
    c. 1964
    d. 1968

5. How many MLB All-Star Games was Darryl Strawberry named to?

    a. 3
    b. 6
    c. 8
    d. 10

6. What year was Darryl Strawberry named the National League Rookie of the Year?

    a. 2001
    b. 2003
    c. 2005
    d. 2007

7. Darryl Strawberry appeared in an episode of *The Simpsons* with several other MLB players.

    a. True
    b. False

8. How many Gold Glove Awards did Darryl Strawberry win during his 17-season MLB career?

    a. 0
    b. 3
    c. 6
    d. 9

9. How many Silver Slugger Awards did Darryl Strawberry win?

    a. 0

    b. 1

    c. 2

    d. 3

10. What is the name of Darryl Strawberry's book that was released in 2017?

    a. Straw: Baseball, Addiction, and Recovery

    b. Darryl Strawberry: My Battle with Addiction

    c. Don't Give Up on Me

    d. Straw

11. How many World Series championships did Darryl Strawberry play for?

    a. 0

    b. 3

    c. 4

    d. 5

12. Darryl Strawberry's full name is Darryl Eugene Strawberry.

    a. True

    b. False

13. How many career home runs did Darryl Strawberry hit during his 17-season MLB career?

    a. 280

    b. 289

c. 301

d. 335

14. What year did Darryl Strawberry lead the National League in home runs with 39?

   a. 1986

   b. 1987

   c. 1988

   d. 1989

15. How many RBI did Darryl Strawberry collect during his 17-season MLB career?

   a. 900

   b. 950

   c. 1,000

   d. 1,050

16. Darryl's older brother, Michael Strawberry, was drafted by the Los Angeles Dodgers.

   a. True

   b. False

17. Darryl Strawberry's son, Darryl Jr. (D.J.), was drafted by which basketball team in the 2007 NBA draft?

   a. Golden State Warriors

   b. Phoenix Suns

   c. Los Angeles Lakers

   d. New York Knicks

18. Which reality show has Darryl Strawberry been on?

    a. The Apprentice
    b. Celebrity Rehab with Dr. Drew
    c. Celebrity Big Brother
    d. Both A & B

19. In his MLB debut, Strawberry played against the Cincinnati Reds. His final game in the MLB was against which team?

    a. Los Angeles Dodgers
    b. Tampa Bay Devil Rays
    c. Colorado Rockies
    d. Boston Red Sox

20. Darryl Strawberry was drafted in the first round, 1st overall by the New York Mets in the 1980 MLB draft.

    a. True
    b. False

QUIZ ANSWERS

1. C – Los Angeles, California

2. A – True

3. C – New York Yankees

4. B – 1962

5. C – 8

6. D – 1983

7. A – True (Third season, "Homer at the Bat")

8. A – 0

9. C – 2

10. C – Don't Give Up on Me

11. C – 4

12. A – True

13. D – 335

14. C – 1988

15. C – 1,000

16. A – True

17. B – Phoenix Suns

18. D – Both A & B

19. B – Tampa Bay Devil Rays

20. A – True

DID YOU KNOW?

1. Darryl Strawberry has appeared on the cover of *Sports Illustrated* seven times. Five of those times were by himself, one was with Dwight Gooden, and the other was with Don Mattingly.

2. Darryl and his wife Tracy started *The Darryl Strawberry Foundation* charity to help children who have autism.

3. Darryl Strawberry opened a Queens restaurant called "Strawberry's Sports Grill" in 2010, It was closed in 2012.

4. Darryl Strawberry was suspended three times by the MLB for substance abuse.

5. Darryl Strawberry was elected to the MLB All-Star Game eight years in a row, from 1984 through 1991. He was the starting NL right fielder in five consecutive All-Star Games.

6. Darryl Strawberry was an analyst for SportsNet New York from 2007 to 2009 as a Mets pre- and post-game anchor.

7. Darryl Strawberry is one of only five MLB players ever to hit two pinch-hit grand slams in the same season.

8. Darryl Strawberry is one of only three MLB players to have played for all four former and current New York teams: the Mets, Yankees, Dodgers, and Giants.

9. Darryl Strawberry wrote a memoir entitled *Straw: Finding My Way*, published in 2009.

10. Darryl Strawberry attended high school at Crenshaw High School. He was drafted out of high school and therefore did not attend college.

CONCLUSION

Learn anything new? Now you truly are the ultimate Mets fan! Not only did you learn about the Mets of the modern era, but you also expanded your knowledge back to the days of the 1969 and 1986 World Series championships.

You learned about the Mets' origins, their history, and where they came from. You learned about the history of their uniforms and jersey numbers, you identified some famous quotes, and read some of the craziest nicknames of all time. You learned more about powerhouse hitters Darryl Strawberry and Mike Piazza. You also learned about pitching ace Tom Seaver. You were amazed by Mets stats and recalled some of the most famous Mets trades and drafts/draft picks of all time. You broke down your knowledge by outfielders, infielders, pitchers, and catchers. You looked back on the Mets' championships, playoff feats, and the awards that came before, during, and after them. You also learned about the Mets' fiercest rivalries, both within their division and out.

Every team in the MLB has a storied history, but the Mets have one of the most memorable of all. They have won two incredible World Series championships with the backing of their devoted fans. Being the ultimate Mets fan takes knowledge and a whole lot of patience, which you tested with this book. Whether you knew every answer or were stumped by several questions, you learned some of the most interesting histories that the game of baseball has to offer.

The deep history of the Mets represents what we all love about the game of baseball. The heart, the determination, the tough times, and the unexpected moments, plus the players who inspire us and encourage us to do our best because, even if you get knocked down, there is always another game and another day.

With players like Pete Alonso, Robinson Cano, and Michael Conforto, the future for the Mets continues to look bright. There is no doubt that this franchise will continue to be one of the most competitive teams in Major League Baseball year after year.

It's a new decade which means there is a clean slate, ready to continue writing the history of the New York Mets. The ultimate Mets fan cannot wait to see what's to come for their beloved Mets.

Made in United States
North Haven, CT
17 March 2023

34182017R00091